dance ideas

age 5–11

101

Also available from A & C Black

101 Youth Fitness Drills – Age 7–11
John Shepherd and Mike Antoniades

101 Youth Fitness Drills – Age 12–16
John Shepherd and Mike Antoniades

101 Youth Athletics Drills
John Shepherd

cush jumbo and roger hurn

dance ideas

age 5–11

A&C

Published by
A & C Black Publishers Ltd
36 Soho Square
London W1D 3QY
www.acblack.com

First edition 2010

ISBN 978 14081 2403 1

A CIP catalogue record for this book is available from the British Library.

Acknowledgements
Photographs and DVD supplied by bebegigi limited
Designed by James Watson
Commissioned by Charlotte Croft
Edited by Kate Turvey

This book is produced using paper that is made from wood grown in managed, sustainable forests. It is natural, renewable and recyclable. The logging and manufacturing processes conform to the environmental regulations of the country of origin.

Typeset in 10 on 12pt Din Regular by Margaret Brain, Wisbech

Printed and bound in the UK by Martins the Printers

CONTENTS

ACKNOWLEDGEMENTS

Special thanks go to all the teachers we've met who, by their example, are showing that participation in dance can give children, from all backgrounds and walks of life, the confidence, discipline and the belief that they can achieve anything they set their minds to.

In particular, we would like to thank the children and teachers of Ivydale School, London, for all their help with this book. The children's enthusiasm during rehearsals for their show, *Pearlies*, was truly inspirational.

To book Cush Jumbo to come and organise and run a dance INSET for your staff, or a dance workshop with your children, please contact Megan Willis at:

Garricks
Angel House
76 Mallinson Road
London SW11 1BN
Tel: 020 7738 1600 Fax: 020 7801 0088

FOREWORD

In an age when one million British children are extremely overweight and fewer of them take regular exercise, dance provides a practical way in which teachers can do something positive to challenge this. That's why Cush and Roger have written *101 Dance Ideas*. The book is packed with practical, easy to follow dance activities that will get the children active and exercising in a way that is fun for all concerned.

As the principal of the BRIT school, I see on a daily basis just what a positive and motivational impact dancing can have on young people. It not only energises them, but also gives them a constructive and disciplined framework in which to express themselves.

Roger Hurn's vast experience in education and training, united with Cush Jumbo's considerable success as a performing arts practitioner, have combined to create a book that will give children and their teachers a huge confidence boost, a real sense of accomplishment and hours of fun along the way. I recommend it wholeheartedly to anyone who cares about the health and happiness of our children.

Nick Williams
Principal
The BRIT School for Performing Arts and Technology

INTRODUCTION

Dance has never been more popular than it is today – which is good news because dancing is a fantastic way of getting fit and having fun. Better still, most primary school children love to dance. But what can you do as a teacher if you can't dance and have no sense of rhythm? What if you think a rumba is a kind of gooey, sweet cake and that a mambo is a poisonous snake rather than a cool Latin-American dance? Does this mean that the children in your school will have to miss out on all the benefits that dancing brings?

Well, the great news for teachers is that you do NOT have to be a celebrity TV dancer to be able to get your children up and dancing because this book, with its simple, step-by-step format, shows you exactly how it's done. It won't turn you into a prima ballerina, but it will give you all the help and ideas you need to get children actively involved in enjoying dance and reaping all the benefits that dancing bestows. In other words, it's for everyone who wants to get their children dancing but doesn't know how to go about doing it.

So what are the benefits? Well, sadly, the UK is in the grip of an obesity epidemic. If we don't act quickly it's predicted that soon over one million British children will be extremely overweight – and that has terrifying implications for their future health and well-being. But don't despair. Dance provides a practical way in which we, as teachers, can do something positive to combat this rise in childhood obesity. Indeed, *101 Dance Ideas* has been specially written to help you make a real difference to the quality of the health and fitness of the children in your care. That's because the ideas it contains are all concerned with getting children active through the medium of dance – and dancing is a marvellous way for children to burn up excess calories and stay trim.

By regularly taking part in the dance routines in this book your children will:

- Improve their cardiovascular fitness
- Strengthen their muscles and bones
- Increase their blood circulation

Moreover, dancing helps produce endorphins, the 'feel good' chemicals, which lead to an increased feeling of well-being and happiness. And that has to be a good thing in terms of fostering positive attitudes on the part of the children.

But that's not all! Dancing is also a fantastic way of helping your children to develop their cognitive skills by, quite literally, getting them to think on their feet. Research shows that participating in dance activities gives children's brains as well as their bodies a workout. For example, taking part in the dance ideas in this book will help your children to:

- Improve their auditory skills by listening to verbal instructions
- Improve their visual skills by watching demonstrations of the moves
- Improve their memory skills by remembering the steps involved

- Improve their attention skills by concentrating on mastering the moves
- Improve their motor skills by successfully putting the dance ideas into practice

The dance activities provided in *101 Dance Ideas* will also help your children learn how to move with increased grace and poise by improving their control over their bodies and their co-ordination skills.

In short, we believe that mastering the different dance steps provided in this book will give your children a huge confidence boost as well as a real sense of achievement. Best of all, we guarantee that you and they will have an enormous amount of fun in the process.

NB
Many of the activities in this book are inspired by traditional or well-established dances, but are presented here in a simplified version to make them accessible to teachers and children alike.

Suggested Music List

All the music links below begin: **www.amazon.co.uk**
   Alternatively all these songs can be found on itunes. Why not try some current chart tracks or songs connected with some favourite TV programmes?

1–7 Warm-Up – anything upbeat that both you and the class will enjoy.

Circle routines
8   The Tea Dance – *Don't Stop Movin'* by S Club 7
      /dont-stop-movin/dp/B001KU8CAO
9   The Twist – *Twistin' The Night Away* by Sam Cooke
      /Twistin-The-Night-Away/dp/B001KC2ZTG
10 The Farruca – *Farruca Sólo Compás* by Francisco Javier Arriaga Hurtado
      /Farruca-Solo-Compas-Tiempo-120/dp/B001NHFG9Y
11 The Gay Gordons – *The Gay Gordons* by Jim Blair and His Scottish Dance Band
      /The-Gay-Gordons/dp/B002NNNXHO
12 The Elizabethan – *The Gathering of Pescodes* by Paul O'Dette
      /The-Gathering-Of-Pescodes/dp/B001RTLOCO
13 The Spotlight – *Bullet Proof* by La Roux
      /Bulletproof/dp/B002DOFBTG
14 The Moon Stomp – *House of Fun* by Madness
      /House-Of-Fun/dp/B002NS1B8W
15 The Polonaise – *Polonaise* by Lokalnych Chóru
      /Polonaise/dp/B002LD5M9I
16 The Gallop – *William Tell Gallop* by Band of The Blues and Royals
      /William-Tell-Galop-Gallop/dp/B002F59HIY
17 The Snake – *PYT* by Michael Jackson
      /P-Y-T-Pretty-Young-Thing/dp/B0010BGGUC
18 The Star – *Uptight* by Stevie Wonder
      /Uptight-Everythings-Alright/dp/B001LZ768M
19 The Arches – *I'm Gonna Be* by The Proclaimers
      /Im-Gonna-Be-500-Miles/dp/B001J8PA2U
20 The Cake Walk – *Cake Walk* by The University of Michigan Symphony Band
      /Suite-Old-American-Dances-Cake/dp/B001L9Y438
21 The Rugby – *Diamond Rings* by Chipmunk
      /Diamond-Rings-Feat-Emeli-Sande/dp/B002H2WL38

Line routines
22 The Bossa Nova – *Blame It On The Bossa Nova* by Jane McDonald
      /Blame-Bossa-Nova/dp/B002G47ODY
23 The Rain Dance – *Singing In The Rain* (any version that suits)
      /Singin-In-The-Rain/dp/B001LXWWBU
24 The Stomp – *Stronger* by Kanye West
      /Stronger-Made-Famous-Kanye-West/dp/B0031CAOJQ
25 Saturday Night – *Saturday Night* by Whigfield
      /Saturday-Night/dp/B001F401MM

93 The Upside Your Head – *Oops Upside Your Head* by The Gap Band
   /Oops-Upside-Your-Head/dp/B001KEF154
94 The Workout – *Number 1* by Tinchy Stryder
   /Number-1-Feat-N-Dubz/dp/B002H2USNS

95–101 Cool Down – anything that you and the class will enjoy chilling out to. If you are stuck for inspiration why not try some popular classical pieces such as Grieg's Peer Gynt, Morning or Saint-Saens – Aquarium from The Carnival of the Animals.

Before you start dancing

■ Practise makes perfect
We know it sounds obvious, but confidence breeds confidence, so try to find some time to learn and practise your chosen routine at home before teaching it to the children. Seeing you confident with the steps will encourage them to trust in your ability and to be confident themselves.

■ Everyone is a dancer
Don't put too much pressure on yourself or the children to look like 'perfect dancers'. Every person has their own personal style and this should be encouraged. The beautiful thing about dance is it can be done in so many ways, so concentrate on the important things – like enjoying yourselves!

■ Horses for courses
Some of the routines have been recommended as KS1 or KS2 routines. This is only a guideline so feel free to use whichever routines you feel are suitable for your children's abilities. Likewise, if you feel that a KS1 class has mastered the KS1 routines, get them started on the ones for KS2.

■ Don't be self-conscious
When learning something new, especially if a class has never danced before, children can feel very self-conscious. They may giggle at themselves or each other, but this is a completely natural reaction. Encourage the children to keep trying and show them that you're not afraid of looking silly – so they shouldn't be either.

■ Return to routines
Once you have mastered a routine, be sure to return to it a few weeks later so the children can not only test their head memory but also see how their muscle memory works. They'll be surprised at what they can remember.

■ Dress appropriately
New or specifically made dance clothing is not needed, but try to ensure the children wear loose, soft clothing and a pair of soft shoes. A t-shirt or vest, tracksuit bottoms or leggings, and trainers or plimsolls will be fine.

■ Show and tell
Remember that dancing is not only about group movement, but also the movement of the individual. If you spot a child doing something interesting or well then encourage them to show the rest of the class. This is not only a confidence builder, but it's also a way to show the other children that individuality will be praised.

■ Music has meaning
We all have songs that mean something to us or put us in a certain mood and children are no different. So look at the songs suggested for each routine as a

guideline and if you or the children find something else that will fit then try it out. Music is a great motivator so if you don't like it, change it!

▨ Share the knowledge
If this book proves useful to you and you believe in its ethos, then share the knowledge, lend the book to a friend or colleague (or, better still, encourage them to buy their own copy!) and encourage them to get their children dancing too.

▨ Have fun!
And we mean just that. Dance is a challenging activity, mentally and physically, but it should never be a chore. Learning, practising and performing it should be fun for you and the children.

WARMING UP

It is vitally important to warm up before taking part in aerobic exercise like dance. An effective warm-up increases the children's heart rate, speeds up their blood circulation and boosts the oxygen supply to their muscles. This helps prevent them from sustaining injuries. But remember, the purpose of a warm-up is not only to stretch and prepare the muscles in the body, but also to stretch and prepare the mind. Moving to the music and repeating the movements will make learning new steps easier later on.

The warm-up routines in this book are enough to ready any class for dancing. You don't have to do them all, but you should select a few activities that best suit the needs of your children.

Moreover, you don't need to stick to any particular rhythm when doing these warm-ups. Choose any piece of upbeat music that everyone will enjoy. Then move at a speed that suits both you and the class but don't forget, the idea is to 'warm-up' so don't move too slowly!

When you are ready to begin, get the children to find their own space in the room. Within this space they should be able to stretch out both arms and not touch anyone else. You should take a position at the front of the class and ensure all the children can see you from where they stand. Now start the music and let's go!

dance 1 stretching the neck and shoulders (KS1 and KS2)

Stand with your feet slightly wider than shoulder width apart, arms at your sides.

- Moving only your head, gently look up at the ceiling, then down at the floor, look over to the right, then over to the left. Repeat four times.

- Moving only your head, take the right ear towards the right shoulder stretching the left side of the neck. Take the left ear to the left shoulder stretching the right side of the neck. Repeat four times.

- Moving only your shoulders, lift both shoulders up towards your ears and slowly circle them backwards. Repeat four times.

- Lift both shoulders up towards your ears and slowly circle them forwards. Repeat four times.

- Repeat both shoulder movements, but this time more quickly.

dance 2 stretching the arms (KS1 and KS2)

Stand with your feet slightly wider than shoulder width apart, arms relaxed at your sides.

- Moving the right arm only and keeping it straight, slowly circle the arm backwards, making a large circle with the hand. Repeat four times.

- Repeat the movement with the left arm four times, then repeat the movement with both arms, but this time move more quickly.

- Keeping the right arm straight and the left hand on the hip raise the right arm up and over your head reaching towards the left wall until you feel a stretch down your right side. Let the hips swing out to the right slightly.

- Repeat with the other arm (right hand on hip).

- Repeat the whole movement four times.

dance 3 stretching the hips (KS1 and KS2)

Stand with your feet slightly wider than shoulder width apart.

- Placing both hands on your hips and keeping both legs straight, push the hips out to the right until you feel a stretch down the inner left thigh.

- Push the hips out to the left until you feel a stretch down the inner right thigh. Push the hips forwards arching the back slightly, then push the hips backwards leaning forwards slightly.

- Repeat the whole movement four times.

- Keeping both hands on the hips and the legs straight, slowly circle the hips four times clockwise.

- Slowly circle the hips anticlockwise four times.

- Repeat the movement in both directions, but this time more quickly.

dance 4 stretching the spine (KS1 and KS2)

Stand with your feet slightly wider than shoulder width apart.

■ Stretching both arms up to the ceiling and keeping them straight, reach forwards and down until your hands are as close to the ground as possible.

■ Wait here for a count of 20, trying to keep the arms and neck relaxed.

■ Then starting at the bottom of the spine and ending with the head, roll the body up until you are standing again.

■ Repeat four times.

dance 5 stretching the feet (KS1 and KS2)

Stand with your feet slightly wider than shoulder width apart.

- Standing with the feet shoulder width apart, with the arms out to the side for balance if needed, lift the right foot slightly off the floor and circle it four times.

- Change feet and circle the left foot four times.

- Repeat the whole movement four times.

dance 6 raising the heart rate (KS1 and KS2)

When children exercise, their muscles need more oxygen to continue working. By raising the heart rate they are able to supply the muscles with oxygen more quickly.

description: Begin with the feet together, let the arms move naturally with you for this activity.

- Using the right foot, step out to the side.
- Bring the foot back to the centre again.
- Repeat with the left foot.
- Repeat this set of two steps eight times (16 steps altogether).
- March on the spot for eight counts.
- Jog on the spot for eight counts.
- Repeat the routine four times.

- Take three jogs forward counting 1, 2, 3 and jump the feet together on 4, clapping the hands at the same time.
- Repeat the three jogs backward, to the right and to the left.
- Repeat the routine four times.
- Finish the warm-up with 25 jumping jacks – five to the front, five to the right side, five to the back, five to the left side and five to the front again. (A jumping jack is when you jump both feet out to the side, while stretching both arms up and out to the side. Then jump both feet back together, pulling the arms back in at the same time.)

dance 7 a warm-up game (KS1 and KS2)

description: Have all the children face you. Tell them they must do the actions you call out when you begin with the phrase 'Simon says'. They must not carry out the actions if you do not use that phrase.

- Simon says 'jump'.
- Simon says 'wave your hands in the air'.
- Jump.
- Simon says 'shake your right leg'.

Continue playing the game until the children are warmed up and ready to dance!

CIRCLE ROUTINES

Dancing in a circle is probably the most ancient form of dancing. It can be found in cultures all over the world. Circle dances are traditionally performed to celebrate a significant event or happening in a community, such as a marriage or a successful harvest.

Circle dances reflect the mood of the occasion and can be boisterous and energetic or stately and elegant. However, the purpose of a circle dance is to experience the pleasure of combining with others to create a shared sense of belonging.

dance 8 the tea dance (KS2)

---

teaching tip

In the tea dance both circles of dancers are moving simultaneously, but starting with different feet. So, to avoid confusion, take each individual circle through their steps before attempting the dance with both circles.

---

description: Ask the children to find a partner and join one hand.

Ask the children to form one large circle with their peers.

Each pair should stand next to each other facing anti-clockwise around the circle.

There should be a smaller inner circle and a larger outer circle.

Begin with the feet together.

step one (both circles at the same time):

- *Inner circle:* Using the left foot walk forwards on counts 1, 2, 3 and kick with the right foot on count 4.

- *Outer circle:* Using the right foot walk forwards on counts 1, 2, 3 and kick with the left foot on count 4.

- *Inner circle:* Using the right foot walk backwards on counts 5, 6, 7 and jump the feet together on count 8.

- *Outer circle:* Using the left foot walk backwards on counts 5, 6, 7 and jump the feet together on count 8.

step two (both circles at the same time):

- Let go of hands.

- *Inner circle:* Using the left foot take three steps to the left on counts 1, 2, 3 and clap the hands on count 4.

- *Outer circle:* Using the right foot take three steps to the right on counts 1, 2, 3 and clap the hands on count 4.

- *Inner Circle:* Using the right foot take three steps back to your partner on counts 1, 2, 3 and bring the feet together on 4.

- *Outer circle:* Using the left foot take four steps back to your partner on counts 1, 2, 3 and bring the feet together on 4.

feeling confident? At Step Two after the clap, don't walk back to your normal partner, instead walk forwards to the next person. Keep changing until you arrive back at your original partner.

dance 9 the twist (KS2)

The Twist made its first appearance in 1959, the era of Rock n Roll, and was revolutionary as it was the first dance where partners didn't actually make any contact with each other when dancing.

teaching tip

Explain to the children that doing the Twist means acting as though they are pulling a towel from side to side to dry their lower back whilst, at the same time, squashing something under the balls of their feet.

description: Ask the children to form a circle ensuring they can all see you. Begin with the feet together, use the arms to help you twist for this activity.

step one:

- Twist both feet seven times to your right on counts 1–7.
- Clap your hands together on count 8.
- Twist both feet seven times to your left on counts 1–7.
- Clap your hands together on count 8.
- Repeat.

step two:

- Jump to face your right side on count 1.
- Twist both feet seven times to your left on counts 2, 3, 4, 5, 6, 7, 8.
- Jump to face your left side on count 1.
- Twist both feet seven times to your left on counts 2, 3, 4, 5, 6, 7, 8.
- Repeat.

feeling confident? Divide the class into two smaller circles and dance the Twist in groups.

dance 10 farruca (KS2)

The Farruca is a type of Flamenco dance from Asturia in Spain and is a 'heavy footed' dance (i.e. lots of stomping!).

description: Ask the children to form a circle ensuring they can all see you. Begin with the feet together, both hands on the left hip.

There are half counts in this dance counted 'and' – 'one and two and three and four'.

step one:

- Using the right foot step to the right side turning the body towards the left on count 1.
- Using the left foot step back on count 2.
- Using the right foot do a step in place on count 3.
- Scuff the left heel in place on count 'and'.

step two:

- Using the left foot step to the left side turning the body slightly towards the right on count 1.
- Using the right foot step back on count 2.
- Using the left foot do a step in place on count 3.
- Scuff the right heel in place on count 'and'.

feeling confident? Ask the children to find a partner to dance the Farruca with. Remind them they will be moving in opposite directions.

dance 11 gay gordons (KS2)

This dance is named after the Scottish regiment, the Gordon Highlanders. The Regiment was founded in 1794 and recruited soldiers from the north east of Scotland – 200 years later it became part of the new Highland regiment.

description: Ask the children to find a partner and form a circle. Ask the children to turn and face the left so the circle will move clockwise. Partners should stand next to each other creating an inner circle and outer circle. Begin with the feet together holding both hands of your partner but still facing forwards.

step one:

■ *Partner A (Outer Circle)* Using the left foot take three steps forward on counts 1, 2, 3 and tap the right foot forward on count 4.

■ *Partner B (Inner Circle)* Using the right foot take three steps forward on counts 1, 2, 3 and tap the left foot forward on count 4.

■ Using the foot that has been 'tapped' both partners take three steps back on counts 5, 6, 7 and tap the foot back on count 8.

■ Repeat Step One.

step two:

■ *Partner B* raises their right hand and lets go of their left hand.

■ *Partner A* lets go of their right hand and twirls under their partner's raised arm for counts 1–8.

■ Partner B then twirls under Partner A's raised arm for counts 1–8.

feeling confident? Let the As and Bs swap over.

dance 12 the Elizabethan (KS2)

Queen Elizabeth I practised dancing every morning as a form of exercise.

description: Ask the children to form a circle ensuring they can all see you. Begin with the feet together, arms held straight and slightly lifted from your sides.

There are half counts in this routine counted 'and'.

step one:

- Using the right foot step to the right side on count 1.
- Tap the left foot forward on count 2.
- Using the left foot step to the left side on count 3.
- Tap the right foot forward on count 4.
- Repeat Step One for counts 5, 6, 7, 8.

step two:

- Using the right foot step forwards on count 1.
- Using the left foot step forwards and rise up on both toes on count 2.
- Clap the hands together on 'and'.
- Using the right foot step backwards on count 3.
- Using the left foot step backwards on count 4.
- Clap the hands together on 'and'.
- Repeat Step Two.

feeling confident? Ask the children to find a partner and have them dance the Elizabethan facing each other. At Step Two they should clap hands with each other instead of by themselves.

dance 13 spotlight (KS1)

description: Ask the children to form a circle ensuring they can all see you. Begin with the feet together, let the arms move naturally with the body for this activity.

> **teaching tip**
> When couples dance in the centre of the circle make sure the rest of the children in the circle give them plenty of encouragement.

step one:

Everybody in the circle does the following steps continuously:

- Using the right foot step to the right on count 1.
- Bring the left foot to meet the right and clap the hands on count 2.
- Using the left foot step to the left on count 3.
- Bring the right foot to meet the left and clap the hands on count 4.

step two:

Two children will take a turn at being in the centre of the circle, facing each other and doing the following steps:

- Jump the right foot across the left foot on count 1.
- Jump the right foot uncrossed from the left foot on count 2.
- Clap the hands twice on counts 3, 4.
- Repeat Step Two jumping the left foot across the right foot for counts 5, 6, 7, 8.

feeling confident? If the children are confident dancing in pairs let them take turns individually in the centre.

dance 14   moon stomp (KS1 and KS2)

This is a simple up-tempo dance based on Jamaican reggae and ska music.

description: Ask the children to form a circle ensuring they can all see you. Begin with the feet apart, use the arms to help you stomp.

step one:

- Using the right foot take a big moon step forward and bounce both knees twice on counts 1, 2.
- Using the left foot take a big moon step forward and bounce both knees twice on counts 3, 4.
- Repeat Step One for counts 5, 6 and 7, 8.

step two:

- Using the left foot take a big moon step backward and bounce both knees twice on counts 1, 2.
- Using the right foot do the same for counts 3, 4.
- Repeat Step Two for counts 5, 6 and 7, 8.

feeling confident? Play with the number of moon steps you use. For example, try taking eight steps forward.

dance 15 polonaise (KS2)

---

teaching tip
One bar of the music equals the time of three walking steps.

---

description: Ask the children to form a circle ensuring they can see you. Ask the children to turn to face the left so the circle will move clockwise. Begin with the feet together, up on the toes and with the arms outstretched.

There are half counts in this dance counted as 'and'.

step one:

- Using the right foot take three steps forward up on your toes on counts 1, 2, 3.
- Lower the right foot down to the floor and bend both knees on 'and'.

step two:

- Using the left foot take three steps forward up on your toes on counts 1, 2, 3.
- Lower the left foot down to the floor and bend both knees on 'and'.

feeling confident? Ask the children to find a partner and join one hand to dance the Polonaise together from one end of the room to the other.

dance 16   gallop (KS1 and KS2)

description: Ask the children to form a circle ensuring they can all see you. Begin with the feet together, hands on your hips.

There are half counts in this routine counted 'and'.

step one:

- Using the right foot step to the right on count 1.
- Bring the left foot to meet the right on 'and'.
- Using the right foot step to the right on count 2.
- Bring the left foot to meet the right on 'and'.
- Repeat Step One for counts 3-and-4-and-5-and-6.

step two:

- Take two jumps on the spot for counts 7, 8.

step three:

- Now repeat Step One beginning with the left foot.

feeling confident? Ask the children to dance the Gallop in smaller circles of four people.

dance 17 snake (KS1 and KS2)

The Snake in this dance refers to a line of children. The Snake dance is a favourite of American college students celebrating their homecoming parade. Homecoming is an American tradition whereby towns with high schools and colleges come together to welcome back former students with a parade.

description: Ask the children to form a circle ensuring they can see you. Ask the children to turn to face the left so the circle can move clockwise. Ask the children to hold on to the waist of the person in front, with one person as the leader.

step one:

- Tap the right foot out to the right on count 1.
- Bring the right foot in on count 2.
- Tap the left foot out to the left on count 3.
- Bring the left foot in on count 4.

step two:

- Take two jumps forward on counts 5, 6.
- Jump both feet out to the side on count 7.
- Jump both feet back together again on count 8.
- The leader should start off by leading the snake in a circle and they can then play around with where they lead everyone.

feeling confident? Ask the children to form two circles. See if you can intertwine the snakes in and out of each other.

dance 18 star (KS1 and KS2)

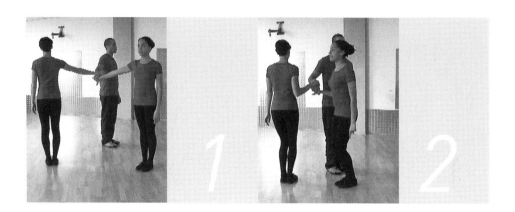

description: Ask the children to form circles of three people. Begin with the feet together, arms at your side. Ask the children to place their right hands into the centre of the circle and hold on.

step one:

■ Using the right foot take eight skips moving forwards around the circle for counts 1–8.

■ Using the right foot take eight skips moving backwards around the circle for counts 1–8.

step two:

■ Using the right foot take a large step to the right on counts 1, 2.

■ Bring the left foot to meet the right on counts 3, 4.

■ Take three mini jumps on counts 5, 6, 7 wait on count 8.

■ Using the left foot take a large step to the left on counts 1, 2.

■ Bring the right foot to meet the left on counts 3, 4.

■ Take three mini jumps on counts 5, 6, 7 wait on count 8.

feeling confident? Ask the children to place their left hand into the centre of the circle and dance the Star in the opposite direction.

description: Ask the children to form two circles one inside the other. Begin with the feet together, hands on hips.

step one:

- *Inner Circle* Using the right foot take eight gallops moving round to the right on counts 1–8.
- *Outer Circle* Using the left foot take eight gallops moving round to the left on counts 1–8.
- Both circles should now reverse the gallops for the next eight counts.

step two:

- *Inner Circle* Using the right foot take eight skips on the spot.
- *Outer Circle* Using the left foot take eight skips on the spot.

step three (both circles simultaneously)

- *Inner Circle* Using the right foot take eight steps backward moving under the arms of the Outer Circle.
- *Outer Circle* Raise your arms high and using the left foot take eight steps forward.

feeling confident? Ask the Inner and Outer Circles to swap over and dance the Arches in their new positions.

dance 20 cake walk (KS1 and KS2)

The Cake Walk originated in the Deep South of the USA. The dance was the only way slaves were allowed to make fun of their owners' aristocratic pretensions. They would perform this routine at their master's house on the plantation and he would judge who had danced the best. A cake was awarded to the winning couple – and this is how the dance got its name.

---

teaching tip
When the children dance the Cake Walk with a partner they must remember to let go of each other's arms when jumping to face the opposite direction. Then they must re-link their arms to jog the other way.

---

description: Ask the children to form a circle ensuring they can all see you. Ask them to turn and face the left so the circle can move clockwise. Begin with the feet together, hands on hips.

step one:
- Using the right foot take 12 large bouncy jogs raising the knees up high in front of you on counts 1, 2, 3, 4, 5, 6, 7, 8 – 1, 2, 3, 4.

step two:
- Take four jumps with the feet together turning clockwise to face the opposite direction for counts 5, 6, 7, 8.

step three:
- Repeat Steps One and Two moving and jumping anti-clockwise.

feeling confident? Ask the children to find a partner and link one arm to dance the Cake Walk around the circle together.

dance 21 rugby (KS2)

description: Ask the children to form a circle ensuring they can all see you. Begin with the feet together, arms linked. The fun part of this routine is trying not to fall over!

> **teaching tip**
> When the children dance the 'Feeling Confident' section of the Rugby with their hands on each other's shoulders they must be careful to stay balanced.

step one:
- Using the right foot step to the right on count 1.
- Kick the left leg forward and diagonally right on count 2.
- Using the left foot step to the left on count 3.
- Kick the right leg forward and diagonally left on count 4.
- Repeat Step One for counts 5, 6, and 7, 8.

step two:
- Drop down onto the right knee on counts 1, 2.
- Change the knees over by dropping onto the left knee on counts 3, 4.
- Change the knees over on count 5, 6.
- Change the knees over on counts 7, 8.

feeling confident? Try the Rugby with the arms resting on each other's shoulders instead of with linked arms.

LINE ROUTINES

Line dances evolved in societies which had a prohibition on men and women dancing together in public. Men and women would dance in separate lines, but today the same dances are usually done in mixed lines.

Line dance routines can take many different forms. For example, some feature pairs of lines in which the dancers face each other, while in others the line forms into a circle, or the line follows a leader around the dance floor. The dancers can maintain contact with their neighbours in a variety of ways. They may hold hands, hold each other's shoulders, or hold on to their neighbour's waist or hips.

Bossa nova means 'new thing' in Portuguese and is the name of a syncopated dance style from Brazil.

---

teaching tip
Point out to the children how the emphasis of the music comes on the second beat in each bar. It will help them tune in to the syncopated rhythm of the dance.

---

description: Ask the children to form lines facing you. Begin with the feet together, hands on hips, or thumbs tucked into the tops of trousers.

step one:

- Using the right foot take three steps to the right on counts 1, 2, 3.
- Tap the left foot on count 4.
- Using the left foot take three steps to the left on counts 5, 6, 7.
- Tap the right foot on count 8.
- Repeat Step One for counts 1–8.

step two:

- Using the right foot step forwards on count 1.
- Cross the left foot over the right foot on count 2.
- Using the right foot step backwards on count 3.
- Using the left foot step to the left on count 4.
- Repeat Step Two for counts 5, 6, 7, 8.

feeling confident? Complete the routine beginning with the left foot instead of the right.

dance 23 rain dance (KS1)

A Rain Dance is actually a ritual dance traditionally performed by rural communities to ensure a plentiful supply of water for their crops. But don't worry – if you use this Rain Dance with your children it is unlikely to result in a week of wet playtimes! It's based on the dance performed by Gene Kelly in the film *Singing in the Rain*.

---

teaching tip
Before you begin, demonstrate what is meant by the phrase 'twinkling the fingers'.

---

description: Ask the children to form lines facing you. Begin with the feet together.

step one:

- Using the right foot take three steps forward whilst raising both arms and twinkling the fingers on counts 1, 2, 3.

- Tap the left foot forward on count 4.

- Using the left foot take three steps backward whilst lowering the arms and twinkling the fingers on counts 5, 6, 7.

- Tap the right foot backward on count 8.

- Repeat Step One.

step two:

- Using the right foot take three steps to the right on counts 1, 2, 3.

- Tap the left foot to the right foot and clap the hands together on count 4.

- Using the left foot take three steps to the left on counts 5, 6, 7.

■ Tap the right foot to the left foot and clap the hands on count 8.

■ Repeat Step Two.

feeling confident? Ask the children to form two lines facing each other and dance the Rain Dance together.

dance 24 stomp (KS1 or KS2)

This routine is based on the American dance style of Stomping. The movements are strong and powerful and are great for raising energy levels and getting rid of frustration and aggression. There are no irregular counts in this routine. Everything is danced on the beat for two bars. Each bar has four beats.

description: Ask the children to find a space in the room facing you. Begin with the feet together, use the arms to help you stomp.

step one:

▪ Using the right foot take three stomps forward on counts 1, 2, 3.

▪ Raise the left knee and tap it with your right hand on count 4.

▪ Using the left foot take three stomps backward on counts 5, 6, 7.

▪ Tap the sole of your right foot with your left hand on count 8.

▪ Repeat Step One.

step two:

▪ Using the right foot, stomp to the right on count 1.

▪ Clap the hands on count 2.

▪ Stomp the left foot on count 3.

▪ Clap the hands on count 4.

▪ Stomp the right foot on count 5.

▪ Tap the sole of the left foot with your right hand on count 6.

▪ Stomp the left foot on count 7.

▪ Tap the sole of the right foot with your left hand on count 8.

▪ Repeat Step Two.

feeling confident? Ask the children to form a circle and dance the Stomp together.

dance 25 saturday night (KS2)

This began life as an aerobic exercise routine. So it is just what you need to help children become more active.

---

teaching tip
Explain the meaning of the word 'rotate' and check that the children know what a 45 degree turn is before attempting the dance. Also explain what you mean by 'both hands making ocean waves' by demonstrating the movement to the children first.

---

description: Ask the children to form lines facing you. Begin with the feet shoulder width apart, arms relaxed.

step one:

- Using both hands do two ocean waves to the right on counts 1, 2.
- Using both hands do two ocean waves to the left on counts 3, 4.
- Hold the right elbow with the left hand and rotate the right wrist on counts 5, 6.
- Hold the left elbow with the right hand and rotate the left wrist on counts 7, 8.

step two:

- Roll the arms downwards and upwards on counts 1, 2, 3, 4.
- Take one step forward on the right foot on count 5.
- Take one step forward on the left foot on count 6.
- Take one step backward on the right foot on count 7.
- Take one step backward on the left foot on count 8.

step three:

- Put the hands on the hips and jump forwards on count 1.
- Keeping the hands on the hips, jump backwards on count 2.
- Jump forwards 45 degrees to the right on count 3.
- Jump backwards 45 degrees to the right and clap the hands on count 4.
- Repeat Steps 1–3 jumping 90 degrees (45+45) each time until you are back where you started.

feeling confident? Ask the children to form two lines facing each other and dance Saturday Night together.

dance 26 | macarena (KS1 and KS2)

La Macarena is a district of Seville and this is where the dance originated in the early 1990s. The Macarena is great for getting groups of children really involved in dance.

---

teaching tip
Check the children know what a 90 degree turn is before you start the dance.

---

description: Ask the children to form lines facing you. Begin with the feet shoulder width apart, arms relaxed.

step one:

- Stretch the right arm out in front of you palm down on count 1.
- Stretch the left arm out in front of you palm down on count 2.
- Turn the right palm up on count 3.
- Turn the left palm up on count 4.

step two:

- Cross the right arm across the chest on count 5.
- Cross the left arm across the chest on count 6.
- Put the right hand behind the head on count 7.
- Put the left hand behind the head on count 8.

step three:

- Place the right hand on the left hip on count 1.

- Place the left hand on the right hip on count 2.

- Place the right hand on the right hip on count 3.

- Place the left hand on the left hip on count 4.

- Move the hips right, left, right on counts 5, 6, 7.

- Jump 90 degrees to the right and clap the hands on count 8.

- Repeat Steps 1–3 jumping 90 degrees each time until you're back to where you started.

feeling confident? Ask the children to form two lines facing each other and dance the Macarena together.

dance 27 the dip (KS2)

The Dip is a dance in the 'funk' style which emphasises a strong rhythmic groove.

---

teaching tip
Explain that a 'walk' in this dance means rolling through the ball of the foot before lowering the heel to the floor.

---

description: Ask the children to form two lines facing you. Begin with the feet together, holding hands along the line.

step one:

- Using the right foot take three walks forward on counts 1, 2, 3.
- Kick the left foot forward on count 4.
- Using the left foot take three walks back on counts 5, 6, 7.
- Jump both feet together on count 8.
- Repeat Step One.

step two:

- The front line now let go of hands and using the right foot take eight steps backward dipping under the arms of the back line on counts 1–8.
- The back line raise their arms (still holding hands) and using the right foot take eight steps forward on counts 1–8.

step three:

- The new back line now join hands, raise arms and using the right foot take eight steps forward on counts 1–8.

■ The new front line now let go of hands and using the right foot take eight steps backward on counts 1–8.

feeling confident?

■ Ask the children to form four lines facing you.

■ Name the lines A, B, C and D.

■ A and B should dance the dip together.

■ C and D should dance the dip together.

dance 28 5, 6, 7, 8 (KS1 and KS2)

This dance was first made popular by a pop group called Steps in the 1990s.

description: Ask the children to form lines facing you. Begin with the feet together and use the arms to help you twist.

step one:

- Twist the feet three times to the right on counts 1, 2, 3.
- Clap the hands on count 4.
- Twist the feet three times to the left on counts 5, 6, 7.
- Clap on count 8.
- Repeat Step One.

step two:

- Take a small step out to the right on count 1.
- Tap the right hip with the right hand on count 2.
- Take a small step out to the left on count 3.
- Tap the left hip with the left hand on count 4.
- Bend the knees on count 5 and pop the hip out to the right on count 6.
- Bend the knees on count 7 and pop the hip out to the left on count 8.
- Repeat Step Two.

feeling confident? Ask the class to make two lines facing each other and dance 5, 6, 7, 8 together.

dance 29 one step (KS2)

description: Get the children to form lines facing you towards the front of the room – this routine will move backwards. Begin with the feet together, hands on the hips or thumbs tucked into tops of trousers.

step one:

- Using the right foot step forwards on count 1.
- Tap the left foot behind the right on count 2.
- Using the left foot take four steps backward on counts 3, 4, 5, 6.
- Using the left foot step to the left on count 7.
- Bring the right foot to meet the left foot on count 8.

step two:

- Using the left foot step forwards on count 1.
- Tap the right foot behind the left on count 2.
- Using the right foot take four steps backward on counts 3, 4, 5, 6.
- Using the right foot step to the right on count 7.
- Bring the left foot to meet the right foot on count 8.

feeling confident? Ask the children to form a circle and dance One Step together.

dance 30 cumbia (KS1 and KS2)

This is a Columbian line dance in 3/4 time which means three beats or counts in each bar. Traditionally, the male dancers dress in white with a red handkerchief around their necks, while the women wear long flowing skirts.

> ### teaching tip
> Explain to the children that most bars of music have either 2, 3 or 4 beats. Play them Baila Esta Cumbia and ask them to clap along in time with it. Then ask them to say how many beats are in each bar of this song (3). This will help them get into the 'feel' and rhythm of the dance.

description: Ask the children to form lines facing you. Begin with the feet together, hands on hips.

step one:

- Using the right foot step backwards and slightly to the left turning the body to the right on count 1.
- Using the left foot step forwards bringing the body back to centre on count 2.
- Bring the right foot to meet the left foot on count 3.
- Remain still on count 4.

step two:

- Using the left foot step backwards and slightly to the right turning the body to the left on count 5.
- Using the right foot step forwards bringing the body back to centre on count 6.
- Bring the left foot to meet the right foot on count 7.
- Remain still on count 8.

feeling confident? Dance the Cumbia in partners. Partner A will dance the original steps. Partner B will begin with the left foot and mirror the steps.

dance 31 the beguine (KS2)

The Beguine is a dance from the islands of Martinique, Cuba and Guadeloupe. It was made famous by Fred Astaire when he danced Begin the Beguine in the movie *Broadway Melody of 1940.*

teaching tip
This dance has half counts counted 'and'.

description: Ask the children to form lines facing you. Begin with the feet together, hands on the hips.

step one:

- Step back on the right foot taking your weight with you on count 1.
- Step forwards on to the left foot taking your weight with you on count 2.
- Using the right foot step to the right on count 3.
- Bring the left foot to meet the right foot on 'and'.
- Using the right foot step to the right again on count 4.

step two:

- Step back on the left foot taking your weight with you on count 5.
- Step forwards on to the right foot taking your weight with you on count 6.
- Using the left foot step to the left on count 7.
- Bring the right foot to meet the left on 'and'.
- Using the left foot step to the left again on count 8.

feeling confident? Ask the children to form two lines facing each other and dance the Beguine together.

dance 32 fandango (KS2)

The Fandango is a lively flamenco-style dance from Portugal. It was very popular with courting couples!

description: Begin with the feet together, knees slightly bent, hands on the hips. When dancing the Fandango try to keep your upper body as still as possible.

step one:

- Tap the right heel forward on count 1.
- Tap the right toe back on count 2.
- Put the right foot down on count 3.

step two:

- Tap the left heel forward on count 1.
- Tap the left toe back on count 2.
- Put the left foot down on count 3.

feeling confident? Ask the children to find a partner and dance the Fandango the traditional way, facing each other.

dance 33 gavotte (KS1 and KS2)

This was originally a 'kissing' dance performed by country people in France. However, when it became popular with the French nobility, flowers were exchanged instead of kisses!

description: Ask the children to form lines facing you. Begin with the feet together, arms held straight and slightly away from the body.

step one:

- Using the right foot step to the right side on count 1.
- Bring the left foot to meet the right on count 2.
- Using the right foot step to the right side again on count 3.
- Point the left foot forward, stretching the whole leg on count 4.

step two:

- Using the left foot step to the left side on count 1.
- Bring the right foot to meet the left foot on count 2.
- Using the left foot step to the left side again on count 3.
- Point the right foot forward, stretching the whole leg on count 4.

feeling confident? Ask the children to form two lines facing each other and dance the Gavotte together.

dance 34 turkey trot (KS1 and KS2)

The Turkey Trot was first danced in San Francisco in 1909. It was a perfect dance for the ragtime jazz music that was becoming popular at the time.

description: Ask the children to form lines facing you. Begin with the feet together. Tuck thumbs under the arms to create turkey wings.

step one:

- Touch the right foot out to the right side on count 1.
- Bring the right foot back to centre on count 2.
- Touch the left foot out to the left side on count 3.
- Bring the left foot back to centre on count 4.
- Repeat Step One for counts 5, 6, 7, 8.

step two:

- Touch the right foot forward on count 1.
- Touch the right foot back on count 2.
- Touch the right foot forward on count 3.
- Bring the right foot back to centre on count 4.
- Repeat Step Two on the left foot for counts 5, 6, 7, 8.

feeling confident? Ask the children to find a partner, join hands and dance the Turkey Trot together.

dance 35 mambo (KS2)

The Mambo dance step originated in Cuba, but its name comes from the island of Haiti, where the Mambo is a voodoo priestess!

description: Ask the children to form columns facing you. Each child should rest their hands on the shoulders of the child in front. The child at the front of each column should let their hands rest on their hips. Begin with the feet together.

step one:

- Using the right foot step forwards rocking the right hip forwards on count 1.
- Using the left foot take a step in place rocking the left hip back on count 2.
- Bring the right foot back to meet the left foot centralising the hips on count 3.
- Remain still on count 4.

step two:

- Using the left foot step back rocking the left hip back on count 1.
- Using the right foot take a step in place rocking the right hip forward on count 2.
- Bring the left foot back to meet the right foot centralising the hips on count 3.
- Remain still on count 4.

feeling confident? Let every child in each column have a go at leading the line, really trying to wiggle the hips!

Hillbillies are so named because they are the descendants of settlers who came from Ulster to make their homes in the Appalachian and Ozarks mountains of the United States. These settlers were supporters of King William and called themselves Billy Boys. As they lived in the mountains they became known as Hillbillies. According to tradition, Hillbillies love raucous and high-spirited dancing.

description: Ask the children to form lines facing you. Begin with the feet together and arms around each other's shoulders.

step one:

- Tap the right heel forward on count 1.
- Changing the feet over, tap the left heel forward on count 2.
- Changing the feet over, tap the right heel forward on count 3.
- Changing the feet over, tap the left heel forward on count 4.
- Repeat Step One for counts 5, 6, 7, 8.
- Jump the feet together on count 8.

step two:

- Using the right foot skip to the right on count 1.
- Using the left foot skip across the right foot on count 2.
- Using the right foot skip to the right on count 3.
- Jump the feet together on count 4.
- Repeat to the left for counts 5, 6, 7, 8.
- Jump the feet together on count 8.

feeling confident? Ask the children to form lines facing each other and dance the Hillbilly routine together.

INTERNATIONAL ROUTINES

The routines in this section are all based on well-known dances from every part of the globe. Whether it's the Highland Fling from Scotland, the Belly Dance from the Middle East or the Bollywood from the Indian sub-continent, each one has a distinctive flavour of the land of its origin.

Indeed, all the dances have been chosen as a celebration of cultural diversity, but the one thing they all have in common is that they are great fun to do. So, it doesn't matter where in the world you live, these routines will unite everyone in the international family of dance.

dance 37 belly dance (KS1)

Belly Dancing as we know it has evolved from traditional women's dances in the Middle East and North Africa. In those days, the men were often not allowed to watch the women dance.

description: Ask the children to find a space in the room facing you. Begin with the feet shoulder width apart, hands on the hips.

step one:

- Bend the right knee twice, pushing the left hip out on counts 1, 2.
- Bend the left knee twice, pushing the right hip out on counts 3, 4.
- Bend the right knee twice, pushing the left hip out on counts 5, 6.
- Bend the left knee twice, pushing the right hip out on counts 7, 8.
- Repeat Step One.

step two:

- Snake the hips in a slow 'figure of eight' movement for counts 1–8 whilst winding the wrists in circles.
- Really try to move the hips and stomach.

step three:

- Repeat Step One for counts 1–8.
- Snake the hips in a quick figure of eight movement whilst turning clockwise for counts 1–8.

feeling confident? Ask the children to form a circle and do the Belly Dance together. Use Step One to move into the circle and out again. Try joining hands as you do the figure of eight.

dance 38 the cossack (KS2)

The Cossacks originally came from the Ukrainian Steppes, north of the Black Sea and the Caucasus Mountains. They were a fiercely independent people. The word Cossack means 'adventurer' and the Cossack dance is very energetic and reflects the Cossack culture.

teaching tip
Make sure the children warm up properly before attempting this dance.

description: Ask the children to find a space facing you. Begin with the feet together and hold the arms out straight to the sides.

step one:

■ Using the right foot take a large step to the right side on count 1.

■ Cross the left foot behind the right foot on count 2.

■ Using the right foot take a large step to the right side on count 3.

■ Cross the left foot in front of the right foot on count 4.

■ Using the right foot take a large step to the right side in count 5.

■ Cross the left foot behind the right on count 6.

■ Using the right foot take a large step to the right side on count 7.

■ Cross the left foot in front of the right foot on count 8.

step two:

■ Using the right foot take four steps turning clockwise to return to the front on counts 1, 2, 3, 4.

- Fold the arms and jump down into a squat on counts 5, 6.

- Jump back up to standing position with the arms out again on counts 7, 8.

- Repeat Step One beginning on the left foot and moving to the left.

- Repeat Step Two using the left foot to turn anti-clockwise.

feeling confident? Try dancing the Cossack in a circle. Let your arms rest on each other's shoulders for Step One. Let go of each other's shoulders for Step Two.

dance 39 cha-cha (KS2)

The Cha-cha is danced by taking very small steps in 4/4 time. 4/4 time means there are four beats (counts) to a bar. The Cha-cha begins with two slower steps and finishes with three quick steps (cha-cha-cha). When dancing the Cha-cha, begin on the second beat of the bar – not the first.

---

teaching tip
You can also count this dance as '2, 3, cha-cha-cha, 2, 3, cha-cha-cha'. That's how the dance got its name!

---

description: Ask the children to find a space facing you. Begin with the feet together, hands on hips. There are half counts in this routine counted 'and'.

step one:

- Remain still for count 1.
- Step back on the right foot taking the weight with you on count 2.
- Transfer the weight forwards onto your left foot on count 3.
- Using the right foot take a small step to the right on count 4 (cha).
- Bring the left foot to meet the right on 'and' (cha).
- Using the right foot take a small step to the right again on count 1 (cha).

step two:

- Remain still on count 1.
- Step forwards on the left foot taking the weight with you on count 2.
- Transfer the weight backwards onto your right foot on count 3.

- Using the left foot take a small step to the left on count 4 (cha).

- Bring the right foot to meet the left on 'and' (cha).

- Using the left foot take a small step to the left again on count 1 (cha).

feeling confident? Ask the children to find a partner and name themselves A and B. Partner A will be dancing Step One first. Partner B will be dancing Step Two first.

dance 40 salsa (KS2)

Salsa comes from Cuba, but it is a fusion of many Latin and Afro-Caribbean dances.

---

teaching tip
The Salsa is danced to four beats using three steps. Each step is one beat long. The last beat in each bar in this Salsa routine is a pause.

---

description: Ask the children to find a space facing you. Begin with the feet together, keep the arms raised at hip height and use them to help you move.

step one:

■ Using the right foot step forwards taking your body weight with you on count 1.

■ Using the left foot take a step in place bringing your weight back on count 2.

■ Bring the right foot to meet the left foot on count 3.

■ Remain still for count 4.

step two:

■ Using the left foot step back taking your body weight with you on count 1.

■ Using the right foot take a step in place bringing your weight back on count 2.

■ Bring the left foot to meet the right foot on count 3.

■ Remain still for count 4.

feeling confident? Ask the children to form a circle and dance the Salsa together.

dance 41 irish jig (KS2)

In eighteenth century Ireland each district had its own dancing master. When dancing masters met at country fairs, they challenged each other to a public dancing contest which only ended when one of them collapsed with exhaustion!

description: Ask the children to find a space in the room facing you. Begin with the feet together, slightly up on your toes. Keep your arms straight and held tightly at your sides.

step one:

- Tap the right heel forward on count 1.
- Tap the right toe back on count 2.
- Hop on the left foot for count 3.
- Set down the right foot behind the left foot on count 4.

step two:

- Tap the left heel forward on count 5.
- Tap the left toe back on count 6.
- Hop on the right foot for count 7.
- Set down the left foot behind the right foot on count 8.
- Repeat Steps One and Two.

feeling confident? Ask the children to form groups of four and make a circle to dance the Irish Jig as a group. The children should try to concentrate on staying together and moving in unison.

dance 42 mazurka (KS2)

The Mazurka is a Polish folk dance in 3/4 time. This means there are three beats or counts in every bar of music.

description: Ask the children to find a space facing you. Begin with the feet together, hands on your hips.

step one:

- Using the right foot step forwards and diagonally to the right on count 1.
- Using the left foot step in front of the right foot on count 2.
- Bring the right foot in behind the left foot on count 3.

step two:

- Using the left foot step forwards and diagonally to the left on count 1.
- Using the right foot step in front of the left foot on count 2.
- Bring the left foot in behind the right foot on count 3.
- Repeat Steps One and Two to move all the way down the room.

feeling confident? The Mazurka is a couple dance, so ask the children to find a partner to dance from one end of the room to the other. Alternatively try dancing round in a circle.

dance 43 tarantella (KS2)

The Tarantella is an Italian folk dance. Legend has it that someone who had been bitten by a tarantula spider could be cured if they danced the Tarentella non-stop. The word 'tarantula' comes from the town of Taranto in southern Italy and was the name given to the European wolf spider found there.

description: Ask the children to find a space facing you. Begin with the feet together and hands on the hips.

step one:

- Using the right foot take four bouncy jogs on the spot for counts 1, 2, 3, 4.
- Using the right foot step to the right on count 5.
- Hop on the right foot and raise the left knee on count 6.
- Using the left foot step to the left on count 7.
- Hop on the left foot and raise the right knee on count 8.
- Repeat Step One.

step two:

- Raise the left arm above your head, put your right hand on your right hip.
- Tap the right heel forward and diagonally to the right twice on counts 1, 2.
- Tap the right toe back and diagonally to the left twice on counts 3, 4.
- Tap the right heel forward and diagonally to the right twice on counts 5, 6.
- Jump the feet together twice and clap the hands twice on counts 7, 8.
- Repeat Step Two beginning with the left foot and raising the right arm above your head.

feeling confident? Ask the children to form one long line and dance the Tarantella. They should try to stay in unison as much as possible.

highland fling (KS2)

The Highland Fling was originally an early medieval war dance from the Scottish Highlands. Victorious warriors would celebrate their success in battle by dancing on their shields.

description: Ask the children to form two lines facing each other. Begin with the feet together, arms above the head as if holding a beach ball.

step one:

- Jump the right foot across the left on count 1.

- Uncross the feet on count 2.

- Jump the left foot across the right foot on count 3.

- Uncross the feet on count 4.

- Repeat Step One for counts 5, 6 and 7, 8.

step two:

- Using the right foot step to the right side on count 1.

- Raise the left knee and hop on the right foot on count 2.

- Using the left foot step to the left side on count 3.

- Raise the right knee and hop on the left foot on count 4.

step three:

- Take four jogs turning clockwise whilst clapping the hands on counts 5, 6, 7, 8.

feeling confident? Use the four jogs in Step Three to turn 180 degrees. You'll now be facing away from the other line. Repeat the Highland Fling using another 180 degree turn to finish facing the opposite line again.

dance 45 bollywood (KS2)

The Bollywood film industry is the largest in the world. Bollywood films are famous for their elaborate musical dance numbers. The dance style incorporates Hip Hop, Jazz, Salsa, East Indian Classical, Folk and Bhangra dancing.

---

teaching tip

This dance entails a good deal of flicking the wrists (or changing the lightbulb) so tell the children to be careful not to flick each other!

---

description: Ask the children to find a space in the room facing you. Begin with the feet together, arms at your sides.

step one:

- Using the right foot step out to the right side raising both arms out to the right and flicking the wrists on count 1.

- Bring the arms and right foot back to centre on count 2.

step two:

- Using the left foot step out to the left side raising both arms out to the left and flicking the wrists on count 3.

- Bring the arms and left foot back to centre on count 4.

- Repeat Steps One and Two for counts 5, 6 and 7, 8.

step three:

- Tap the right foot forward on count 1, whilst flicking the wrists forwards.

- Replace the right foot on count 2.

- Tap the left foot forward on count 3, whilst flicking the wrists higher.

- Replace the left foot on count 4.

- Repeat Step Three for counts 5, 6 and 7, 8 flicking the wrists higher each time.

feeling confident? Ask the children to form a circle to dance the Bollywood together.

dance 46 country dance (KS1 and KS2)

Queen Elizabeth I enjoyed watching and taking part in country dancing, but the first collection of *English Country Dances* wasn't published until 1651. However, it proved so popular that even King Louis XIV of France had a copy!

description: Ask the children to form groups of three, find a space and make a small circle. Begin with the feet together, and use the arms to help you skip.

step one:

- Using the right foot take three skips clockwise on counts 1, 2, 3, 4.
- Using the right foot take three skips backward on counts 5, 6, 7, 8.
- Using the right foot take three skips turning clockwise to end up facing the other way around the circle on counts 9, 10, 11.
- Jump both feet together and clap the hands on count 12.
- Repeat Step One using the left foot.

step two:

- Placing the right hand into the centre of the circle and holding on, use the right foot to take 11 skips around the circle clockwise for counts 1–11.
- Jump the feet together on count 12, turning to face the other way and letting go of right hands.
- Placing the left hand into the centre of the circle and holding on, use the left foot to take 11 skips around the circle anti-clockwise for counts 1–11.
- Jump both feet together on count 12, turning to face the other way and letting go of right hands.

feeling confident? Ask the class to form one large circle for the country dance routine. At Step Two place the right hand on the right shoulder of the person in front of you.

dance 47 kenyan hop (KS1 and KS2)

This routine is inspired by the dance performed by the young men of the Masai tribe to celebrate their bravery after going on a lion hunt. This dance is brilliant for strengthening the legs.

description: Ask the children to find a space facing you. Begin with the feet together, arms tightly at your sides. This routine is danced over 8 counts.

step one:

■ Take eight high jumps on the spot for counts 1–8 keeping the legs tightly together and straight in the air.

step two:

■ Using the right foot take four high hops for counts 1–4.

■ Using the left foot take four high hops for counts 5–8.

step three:

■ Using the right foot, step to the right side on count 1 so the feet are shoulder width apart.

■ Bounce both knees for counts 2–8, relaxing the arms.

■ Repeat Steps One, Two and Three.

feeling confident? Ask the children to form a large circle and take turns doing the Kenyan hop in the middle in pairs. Everybody in the circle should bounce (see Step Three) as the dancers in the middle hop.

dance 48 polka (KS2)

The Polka is a light bouncy dance from Central Europe. It is in 3/4 time (three beats to each bar) and is counted 1, 2, 3–1, 2, 3–1, 2, 3–1, 2, 3.

> **teaching tip**
> Demonstrate to the children that a 'mini' step is a third of the size of a normal step.

description: Ask the children to find a space facing you. Begin with the feet together, hands behind your back.

step one:

▪ Using the right foot step forwards on count 1, bending both knees slightly.

step two:

▪ Using the left foot take a mini step forward on count 2.

step three:

▪ Using the right foot take a mini step forward on count 3.

▪ Now repeat the whole routine beginning with the left foot.

feeling confident? The Polka is a progressive dance so try spreading out and using the steps to move clockwise around the room. It can also be a partner dance so put the children into pairs. They should hold hands and see if they can dance around the room together staying in time.

The Limbo comes from the Caribbean island of Trinidad. The word 'limbo' is based on the English word 'limber' and, in this case, means being supple and able to bend the body easily.

> **teaching tip**
> Demonstrate to the children how to 'shimmy' the shoulders before starting the dance.

description: Ask the children to find a space facing you. Begin with the feet together, and use the arms to help you move.

There are half counts in this routine counted 'and'.

step one:

- Using the right foot step to the right on count 1.
- Cross the left foot over the right foot on count 2.
- Using the right foot step to the right on count 3.
- Double clap on 'and 4'.
- Shimmy the shoulders down on counts 5, 6.
- Shimmy the shoulders up on counts 7, 8.
- Repeat Step One to the left on counts 1–8.

step two:

- Twist down to the floor waving the arms from left to right four times on counts 1, 2, 3, 4.

■ Twist back to standing whilst waving the arms left to right four times on counts 5, 6, 7, 8.

■ Repeat Step Two.

feeling confident? Ask the children to form a carnival group consisting of lines of three people – they should begin the routine at one end of the room and work their way to the other.

dance 50   rumba (KS2)

The word 'rumba' comes from the Spanish verb 'rumbear' which means going out partying, dancing and having a good time.

---

teaching tip
Begin this dance on the second count of the music, counting 2, 3, 4, 1–2, 3, 4, 1.

---

description: Ask the children to find a space facing you. Begin with the feet together, hands on your hips.

step one:
- Using the right foot step backwards on count 2, taking your weight with you.
- Using the left foot step forwards on count 3, taking your weight with you.
- Using the right foot step to the right on count 4.
- Remain still on count 1.

step two:
- Using the left foot step forwards on count 2, taking your weight with you.
- Using the right foot step backwards on count 3, taking your weight with you.
- Using the left foot step to the left on count 4.
- Remain still on count 1.

feeling confident? Ask the children to find a partner and dance the Rumba together. Partner A will dance the original routine and Partner B will begin by stepping forward on the left foot.

CONTEMPORARY ROUTINES

When someone asked the famous dancer Isadora Duncan what contemporary dance was all about she replied: 'If I could tell you that, I wouldn't have to dance it.' In fact it arose as a reaction against the straightjacket imposed on dance by traditional ballet. Therefore, contemporary dance is distinguished by its adaptability and it can be danced to almost any type of music. Moreover, it can be combined with other dance forms to make new ways of moving to music.

The 15 routines in this section have been chosen to reflect recent dance trends that complement the fluid and natural movements that characterise contemporary dance.

dance 51 disco (KS1 and KS2)

You can bring *Saturday Night Fever* to your school any day of the week with this upbeat dance routine. It's fun to do and uses the steady 'four-to-the-floor' beat typical of 1970s disco music.

> **teaching tip**
> When the children jump and clap it should be one fluid movement, not two separate actions.

description: Ask the children to find a space in the room facing you. Begin with the feet together, let the arms move naturally with your body.

step one:

- Using the right foot step to the right on count 1.
- Using the left foot step across the right foot on count 2.
- Using the right foot step to the right again on count 3.
- Jump both feet together and clap the hands on count 4.
- Repeat Step One to the left on counts 5, 6, 7, 8.

step two:

- Using the right foot take three steps turning to the right on the counts 1, 2, 3.
- Clap the hands and jump both feet together to face the front on count 4.
- Using the left foot take three steps turning to the left on counts 5, 6, 7.
- Clap the hands and jump both feet together to face the front on count 8.
- Repeat Step Two.

feeling confident? Split the children into two groups and dance the Disco one group at a time.

dance 52 boogaloo (KS1)

This dance was really popular in the 1960s.

teaching tip
Dancing the Boogaloo is all about isolating designated parts of the body – so encourage the children to try to keep the rest of their body still as they move the named body part. It's not as easy as it sounds!

description: Ask the children to find a space facing you. Begin with the feet shoulder width apart, arms relaxed.

step one:

- Flick the right hand upwards on count 1.
- Flick the left hand upwards on count 2.
- Bending the left knee push the right hip out to the side on count 3.
- Bending the right knee push the left hip out to the side on count 4.

step two:

- Tip the head to the right on count 5.
- Tip the head to the left on count 6.
- Lift up both shoulders on count 7.
- Lower both shoulders on count 8.

feeling confident? Speed up the moves and try to connect them together as smoothly as possible.

dance 53 moonwalk (KS2)

This dance was popularised by Michael Jackson, although he was not the first entertainer to use the technique. The dance creates the impression that the dancer is moving forward while they are, in fact, going backwards.

---

teaching tip

This is a difficult move and takes a good deal of practice to master. The trick is to link all four moves together smoothly until they become one fluid movement. Dancing the Moonwalk in socks can help the children to achieve this.

---

description: Ask the children to find a space facing you. Begin with the feet together, use your arms to help you balance.

- Lift the right heel off the floor transferring the weight onto the left foot, but keeping the ball of the right foot in contact with the floor on count 1.
- Slide the left foot backwards keeping it in full contact with the floor on count 2.
- Flatten the right foot and lift the left heel off the floor transferring the weight onto the right foot on count 3.
- Slide the right foot backwards keeping it in full contact with the floor on count 4.
- Repeat Step One.

feeling confident? Try dancing the Moonwalk wearing shoes.

dance 54 tap stamp (KS1 and KS2)

Tap dance is an American innovation in dancing which involves rhythmic tapping of the feet.

> **teaching tip**
> It is important to wear covered shoes for this routine so that all the sounds can be heard.

description: Ask the children to find a space facing you. Begin with the feet together, use your arms to help you tap stamp.

step one:

- Using the right foot step to the right on count 1.
- Bring the left foot to meet the right foot on count 2.
- Using the right foot step to the right on count 3.
- Stamp the left foot forward on count 4.
- Repeat the above moves on counts 5, 6, 7, 8, but lead with the left foot this time.
- Repeat the whole of Step One.

step two:

- Stamp the right foot forward angling the toes inward on count 1.
- Pivoting on the heel turn the toes outward to the right on count 2.
- Pivoting on the heel turn the toes inward on count 3.
- Pivoting on the heel turn the toes outwards on count 4.
- Repeat the above moves on counts 5, 6, 7, 8, but lead with the left foot.
- Repeat the whole of Step Two.

feeling confident? Ask the children to form a circle and dance the Tap Stamp together.

dance 55 jazz (KS2)

Jazz dancing evolved in the USA as part of the African-American cultural tradition. It is noted for its improvised nature and is heavily influenced by the rhythms and syncopated feel of jazz music.

> **teaching tip**
> Start well back as this routine moves forward.

description: Ask the children to find a space facing you. Begin with the feet together, and let your arms move naturally with your body.

There are half counts in this routine counted 'and'.

step one:

- Using the right foot step forward on count 1.
- Tap the ball of the left foot directly behind the right foot and transfer the weight onto it on 'and'.
- Using the right foot step forward again on count 2.

step two:

- Using the left foot step forwards on count 3.
- Tap the ball of the right foot directly behind the left foot and transfer the weight onto it on 'and'.
- Using the left foot step forwards again on count 4.
- Repeat Steps One and Two for counts 5 'and' 6, 7 'and' 8.
- This movement is called a step ball change.

feeling confident? Ask the children to find a partner and line up at one end of the room to dance the Jazz routine moving down the room in pairs. They should try to make the steps flow together.

dance 56 the strut (KS2)

The Strut is a type of dance that was popular when jazz was all the rage. It's similar in style to what young African-Americans today call 'stepping'.

teaching tip
Explain to the children that the verb 'to strut' means to walk proudly or haughtily. Knowing this will help them get the feel of the dance.

description: Ask the children to find a space facing you. Begin with the feet together, and use the arms to help you strut.

step one:

- Using the right foot step forwards on count 1.
- Clap the hands on count 2.
- Using the left foot step forwards on count 3.
- Clap the hands on count 4.
- Repeat Step One for counts 5, 6, 7, 8.

step two:

- Using the right foot strut forwards and throw the right arm out to the right on count 1.
- Using the left foot strut forwards and throw the left arm out to the left on count 2.
- Using the right foot strut forwards and throw the right arm up high on count 3.
- Using the left foot strut forwards and throw the left arm up high on count 4.

- Using the right foot take two steps forward and throw the arms down on counts 5, 6.

- Jump the right foot across the left foot and pull the arms in on count 7.

- Twist the body anti-clockwise to face the other way on count 8.

- Repeat Steps One and Two.

feeling confident? Divide the class into two groups and ask each group to begin at an opposite end of the room. They should dance the Strut moving towards each other and then moving away.

dance 57 break dance (KS2)

This is an acrobatic and very energetic style of solo dancing to hip hop and rap music. Break dancing started in the United States in the 1980s.

> **teaching tip**
> The children will need to have a large personal space to do break dancing as it entails a great deal of vigorous movement.

description: Ask the children to find a space facing you. Begin with the feet together, arms relaxed.

step one:

- Jump down into a crouch, hands on the floor shoulder width apart on counts 1, 2.
- Jump the right leg back keeping both hands on the floor and the left knee bent on count 3.
- Jump the left leg back to join the right leg on count 4.
- Jump both feet forward getting back to crouch position on counts 5, 6.
- Transfer the weight onto the hands and do a high bunny hop with both feet up into the air on counts 7, 8.

step two:

- Jump both feet out to the sides straightening the legs and leaving the hands on the floor on counts 1, 2.
- Standing up straight, jump the right foot forward and the left foot back whilst pumping the arms on count 3.

- Change the feet over on count 4.
- Using the right foot step forwards on count 5.
- Kick the left foot forward whist clapping the hands on count 6.
- Using the left foot step back on count 7.
- Jump the feet together on count 8.

feeling confident? Ask the children to form a circle and break dance two at a time facing each other in the centre.

dance 58   the battle (KS2)

In this dance, the dancers battle to outdo each other with their moves. One of the moves is the 'walk'. It is the most basic dance move. Walks are like normal walking steps, but they reflect the nature of the dance. So, in this case, the walks need to be very heavily grounded and expressive.

description: Ask the children to find a partner and a space. Begin with the feet together, arms relaxed facing your partner. Use your arms to help you complete each move.

There are half counts in this routines counted 'and'.

Partner A dances a step first, then Partner B repeats the step until the routine is complete.

step one:
- ▥ Jump on the spot on count 1.
- ▥ Using the right foot step out to the right on count 2.
- ▥ Now Partner B repeats.

step two:
- ▥ Tap both knees with both hands for count 3.
- ▥ Cross the hands across the chest on count 'and'.
- ▥ Jump the feet together and stretch both arms out to the side on count 4.
- ▥ Now Partner B repeats.

step three:
- ▥ Jump down to a crouch on count 5.
- ▥ Jump up to standing on count 6.

- Take three walks backward on counts 7 'and' 8.

- Now Partner B repeats.

feeling confident? Divide the class into two groups and name them A and B. The two groups dance the Battle together, moving further away each time. Ask the groups to take turns to add extra moves as a challenge to each other.

dance 59 street jam (KS2)

Street Jam is influenced by the informal high-energy hip hop dances performed on the streets of American cities by enthusiastic groups of young dancers.

description: Ask the children to find a space facing you. Begin with the feet shoulder width apart, and arms relaxed – let your arms move naturally with the body.

step one:

- Stretch the right arm forward on count 1.
- Stretch the left arm forward on count 2.
- Using the right foot step out to the right on count 3.
- Using the left foot step out to the left on count 4.

step two:

- Jump the right foot across the left foot stretching both arms out to the sides on count 5.
- Turn the whole body anti-clockwise bringing the arms in tight to the body until you reach the front again on count 6.
- Using the right foot take a large step forward on count 7.
- Bring the left foot to meet the right foot and clap the hands on count 8.

feeling confident? Divide the class into two groups and take turns dancing the Street Jam.

dance 60 rock star (KS1)

These days it seems that everyone wants to be a rock star! And it doesn't matter if you have no musical ability – you can still play air guitar. In fact, there is an Air Guitar World Championship held every year in Finland. This Rock Star dance takes that event as its inspiration and gives you and the children the chance to act the part of a heavy metal rock god or goddess!

description: Ask the children to find a space facing you. Begin with the feet shoulder width apart, arms relaxed.

step one:

- Drum the right heel strongly eight times pointing the right finger high in the air for counts 1–8.
- Drum the left heel strongly eight times pointing the left finger high in the air for counts 1–8.
- Repeat Step One.

step two:

- Holding your air guitar strum it with the right hand eight times for counts 1–8.
- Strum the air guitar eight times with the right hand whilst jumping eight times on counts 1–8.
- Strum the air guitar with the right hand eight times whilst jumping eight times clockwise on counts 1–8.
- Strum the air guitar with the right hand eight times whilst jumping eight times anti-clockwise on counts 1–8.

feeling confident? Ask the children to form two lines facing each other and dance the Rock Star together.

dance 61 show dance (KS2)

A Show Dance is one that, as its name implies, is usually performed for an audience. This particular show dance would be suitable for an assembly or at a dance performance for parents.

description: Ask the children to find a space facing you. Begin with the feet together, arms relaxed. Start slightly back as this routine will move forwards.

step one:

- Using the right foot step forwards on count 1.
- Hop high on the right foot whist raising the left knee and stretching the right arm into the air on count 2.
- Using the left foot take two walks forward on counts 3, 4.
- Using the left foot step forwards on count 5.
- Hop high on the left foot whilst raising the right knee and stretching the left arm into the air on count 6.
- Using the right foot take two walks forward on counts 7, 8.
- Repeat Step One.

step two:

- Using the right foot step to the right on count 1.

- Bring the left foot to meet the right foot on count 2.

- Using the right foot step to the right and bend the right knee deeply, whilst stretching the right arm up and diagonally right, and the left arm down and diagonally left, while also twinkling the fingers on counts 3, 4.

- Repeat Step Two but in reverse, stepping left with the left foot, bending the left knee deeply and stretching the left arm up and diagonally left, and the right arm down and diagonally right for counts 5, 6 and 7, 8.

- Repeat the whole of Step Two.

feeling confident? Ask the children to form a circle and dance the Show Dance moving around the circle. They should try to stay together and perform as a troupe.

dance 62 pop star (KS2)

This dance is inspired by the type of dance routines seen on pop music TV channels.

> **teaching tip**
> Make sure the children know what a 90 degree turn is before starting the routine.

description: Ask the children to find a space facing you. Begin with the feet together, use your arms to help you move.

step one:

- Using the right foot step to the right on count 1.
- Tap the ball of the left foot behind the right foot on count 2.
- Using the left foot step to the left on count 3.
- Tap the ball of the right foot behind the left foot on count 4.
- Repeat Step One.

step two:

- Using the right foot take three walks forward on counts 1, 2, 3.
- Jump the feet out shoulder width apart on count 4.
- Lift the right shoulder up to the right ear on count 5.
- Drop the right shoulder and lift the left shoulder on count 6.
- Drop the left shoulder and lift the right shoulder on count 7.
- Jump the feet back together and clap the hands on count 8.

feeling confident? At the end of Step Two, jump the feet back together whilst turning 90 degrees to the left, then repeat the whole routine facing the new direction. Keep jumping 90 degrees at the end of each repetition until you end up where you started.

dance 63 nu rave (KS2)

Nu Rave is usually danced to electro trance 'indie' styles of music.

---

teaching tip
Warn the children that when they are dancing the Nu Rave with a partner, they will be moving in opposite ways to each other.

---

description: Ask the children to find a space facing you. Begin with the feet together, arms relaxed.

step one:

- Stretch the right arm forward on count 1.
- Stretch the left arm forward on count 2.
- Cross the right arm in front of the left arm on count 3.
- Cross the left arm in front of the right arm on count 4.

step two:

- Using the right foot take a step out to the right whilst pushing both hands out to the right on count 5.
- Bring the right foot back to centre and arms down on count 6.
- Using the left foot take a step out to the left whilst pushing both hands out to the left on count 7.
- Bring the left foot back to centre and arms down on count 8.

feeling confident? Ask the children to find a partner to dance the Nu Rave opposite each other. Encourage them to make the movements crisp and sharp.

dance 64 the slam (KS1)

Slam dancing is a form of bonding for those who do it together at live music performances. It is also an excellent way of releasing pent up energy and frustration.

> **teaching tip**
> This is a fairly boisterous dance so make sure the children have plenty of space in which to dance.

description: Ask the children to find a space facing you. Begin with the feet together, let the arms move naturally with you.

step one:

- Using the right foot take three skips forward on counts 1, 2, 3.
- Jump both feet wide apart, bending the knees deeply and stretching out the arms and fingers to the sides on count 4.
- Using the right foot take three skips backward on counts 5, 6, 7.
- Jump both feet wide apart, bending the knees deeply and stretching out the arms and fingers to the sides on count 8.

step two:

- Using the right foot take three skips to the right on counts 1, 2, 3.
- Jump both feet wide apart, bending the knees deeply and stretching the arms and fingers to the side on count 4.
- Using the left foot take three skips to the left on counts 5, 6, 7.
- Jump both feet wide apart, bending the knees deeply and stretching the arms and fingers out to the sides on count 8.

feeling confident? Ask the children to form a circle and dance the Slam facing each other.

dance 65 the mosh (KS1)

'Moshing' is a very active type of dance and is typically done in the space in front of the stage which is known as the mosh pit.

description: Ask the children to find a space facing you. Begin with the feet together, arms held tightly to your sides.

- Take eight little jumps on the spot for counts 1–8.
- Take eight little jumps moving forwards for counts 1–8.
- Take eight little jumps moving to the right for counts 1–8.
- Take eight little jumps turning clockwise for counts 1–8.
- Take eight little jumps moving to the left for counts 1–8.
- Take eight little jumps turning anti-clockwise for counts 1–8.
- Take eight little jumps moving backwards for counts 1–8.
- Take eight little jumps on the spot for counts 1–8.

feeling confident? Ask the children to find a partner and join hands to dance the Mosh together. This is very good for getting the heart rate up so don't be afraid to try faster music.

TRADITIONAL ROUTINES

From the time when the first cave dwellers clapped their hands, shuffled their feet and began to move rhythmically, people have expressed themselves through dance. Since those early days, a huge variety of dance forms have evolved. However, in this section, we are focusing on routines inspired by dances that have become an integral and instantly recognisable part of the traditional world of dance.

A Barn Dance must have a 'caller'. The caller (you) explains all the steps beforehand and then calls them out again as the music plays.

---

teaching tip

Go through the dance with the children step-by-step before attempting it with the music and the call.

---

description: Ask the children to make two lines facing each other. They should each be opposite a partner and be no more than two feet apart. Decide which end of the two lines is the 'top' – this will be important later. Begin with the feet together and use your arms to help you move.

There are half counts in this dance counted 'and'.

step one:

- Using the right foot take three steps forwards on counts 1, 2, 3.
- Using the left foot first stamp twice on counts 'and' 4.
- Using the left foot first take three steps backwards on counts 5, 6, 7.
- Using the right foot first stamp twice on counts 'and' 8.
- Repeat Step One.

step two:

- Taking right hands with your partner skip clockwise on counts 1–8.
- Taking left hands with your partner skip anti-clockwise on counts 1–8.

- Taking both hands with your partner skip clockwise on counts 1–8.
- Keeping hold of both hands skip anti-clockwise on counts 1–8.

step three:

- The first pair at the top of the line join hands with each other.
- Everyone else takes one step back from their partner.
- The first pair take eight skips down the centre of the two lines while everyone else claps along for counts 1–8.
- The first pair take eight skips back to the top of the line while everyone else claps along for counts 1–8.

Repeat the Barn Dance from Step One.

At Step Three let the next pair take their turn skipping down the middle.

feeling confident? Ask each pair to make up a freestyle movement – for example, they could hop up on their right foot and back on their left foot. They can do this together down the middle of the two lines at Step Three.

dance 67 the carioca (KS2)

A Carioca is the name given to an inhabitant of Rio de Janeiro, Brazil. The Carioca dance is similar to the Samba and was made famous by Fred Astaire and Ginger Rogers in the film *Flying Down to Rio*. Fred and Ginger danced the Carioca with their foreheads touching.

teaching tip
It is definitely worth asking the children to practise touching foreheads and resting hands on shoulders before starting the dance. Try to keep all steps small.

description: Ask the children to find a partner and get into a space facing them. The children should touch foreheads for the whole routine. They should also rest both hands on each other's shoulders to reduce pressure. Partner A will dance Step One first and then Step Two. Partner B will dance Step Two first and then Step One.

step one:

- Using the right foot take a small step to the right on count 1.
- Place the left foot behind the right foot on count 2.
- Using the right foot take a small step to the right on count 3.
- Bring the left foot to meet the right foot on count 4.

step two:

- Using the left foot take a small step to the left on count 5.
- Place the right foot behind the left foot on count 6.
- Using the left foot take a small step to the left on count 7.
- Bring the right foot to meet the left foot on count 8.

feeling confident? Ask the children to form groups of four and dance the Carioca with all four foreheads touching, with hands on each other's shoulders. Tell the children to be careful to take the majority of the pressure on each other's arms.

dance 68 hula hula (KS1)

Hula dancing is from Hawaii. It originated as a form of worship during religious ceremonies, but it slowly evolved into the form of entertaining dancing we all know today.

description: Ask the children to find a space facing you. Begin with the feet shoulder width apart, arms relaxed.

step one:

- Using the right foot step to the right and ripple the arms once like a wave to the right on count 1.
- Bring the left foot to meet the right foot and ripple the arms once like a wave to the right on count 2.
- Using the right foot step to the right and ripple the arms once like a wave on count 3.
- Tap the left foot, bring it to meet the right foot and ripple the arms once like a wave on count 4.

step two:

- Using the left foot step to the left and ripple the arms once on count 5.
- Bring the right foot to meet the left foot and ripple the arms once on count 6.
- Using the left foot step to the left and ripple the arms once on count 7.
- Tap the right foot, bring it to meet the left foot and ripple the arms once on count 8.

feeling confident? Ask the children to form two long lines facing each other to dance the Hula Hula together. Remind them the lines will be moving in opposite directions.

dance 69 lambeth walk (KS2)

The Lambeth Walk is a show-stopping song from the musical *Me and My Girl*. The song gave rise to a popular walking dance, done in a jaunty cockney style.

description: Ask the children to find a partner and get into a space facing you. Begin with the feet together, one arm linked. Both partners will dance the same steps.

step one:

- Using the right foot take three steps forward on counts 1, 2, 3.
- Tap the left heel forward on count 4.
- Using the left foot take three steps back on counts 5, 6, 7.
- Tap the right toe back on count 8.

step two:

- Using the right foot step to the right on count 1.
- Cross the left foot in front of the right foot on count 2.
- Using the right foot step to the right on count 3.
- Kick the left foot to the right on count 4.

step three:

- Using the raised left foot step to the left on count 5.
- Cross the right foot in front of the left foot on count 6.
- Using the left foot step to the left on count 7.
- Kick the right foot to the left on count 8.

feeling confident? Ask the children to make one long line and link arms to dance the Lambeth Walk together.

dance 70 waltz (KS2)

The Waltz is a simple dance performed in 3/4 time. When you count the beat to waltz music, you'll be counting '1–2–3 and 1–2–3 and 1–2–3.'

> **teaching tip**
> The children should never look at their feet when dancing the Waltz. If they do they are bound to step on somebody else's toes! In fact, when they waltz with a partner they should stand with their right foot aimed between their partner's feet.

description: The children will dance the steps solo. Begin with the feet together, hands on your hips.

step one:

- Using the right foot take a step forward on count 1.
- Using the left foot take a step to the left, rising up onto the toes of both feet, and drag the right foot in to meet the left on count 2.
- Lower both feet down to flat on count 3.

step two:

- Using the left foot take a step forward on count 1.
- Using the right foot take a step to the right on count 2.
- Lower both feet down to flat on count 3.

feeling confident? Ask the children to find a partner and join hands to dance the Waltz together. One partner will dance the waltz steps backwards.

dance 71 the jive (KS2)

The Jive is a dance style from the USA based on a simple 6-beat sequence – slow/two beats, slow/two beats, quick/one beat, quick/one beat.

> **teaching tip**
> The jive is danced over 6 counts of music. Listen to the music and count 1 and 2, 3 and 4, 5, 6, 1 and 2, 3 and 4, 5, 6.

description: Get the children to find a space in the room facing you. Begin with the feet together, the knees slightly bent. Use the arms to help you move.

This dance has half counts in this routine counted 'and'.

step one:

- Using the right foot take a small step to the right on count 1.
- Bring the left foot to meet the right foot on count 'and'.
- Using the right foot take a small step to the right on count 2.
- Using the left foot take a small step to the left on count 3.
- Bring the right foot to meet the left foot on count 'and'.
- Using the left foot take a small step to the left on count 4.

step two:

- Using the right foot take a small step behind the left foot on count 5.
- Raise the left foot and place it down on count 6.

feeling confident? Ask the children to find a partner and join hands to dance the Jive together. One partner will begin with the left foot instead of the right.

dance 72 morris dance (KS2)

No-one really knows the origins of the Morris Dance. Some say it has its roots in the 14th century 'Fool's Dance' in which the dancers dressed like court jesters. Others believe that it is a far older 'magical' dance and the bells, waving handkerchiefs, and clashing sticks were intended to ward off evil spirits. Whatever the real explanation, this simple Morris Dance is just for fun.

description: Ask the children to form two lines facing each other. Make sure each child is facing a partner and standing at least two metres apart. Begin with the feet together, and use your arms to help you move.

There are half counts in this routine counted 'and'.

step one:

- Using the right foot step forwards on count 1.
- Raise the left foot and hop on the right foot on count 'and'.
- Using the left foot step forwards on count 2.
- Raise the right foot and hop on the left foot on count 'and'.
- Repeat Step One for counts 3 'and'.
- Jump the feet together on count 4.

step two:

- Slap right hands with your partner on count 5.
- Clap your own hands together on count 6.
- Slap left hands with your partner on count 7.
- Clap your own hands together on count 8.

step three:

- Using the right foot take three skips backward on counts 1–3.
- Jump the feet together on count 4.
- Slap both knees with both hands on counts 5, 6.
- Clap the hands together on counts 7, 8.

feeling confident? At Step Two, tap right and left feet with your partner instead of hands.

dance 73 the charleston (KS2)

This dance is synonymous with the 'Roaring 20s' and ragtime jazz. However, it was first danced in the early years of the 20th century by African-Americans who lived on an island off the coast of Charleston, South Carolina.

description: Begin with the feet together, knees slightly bent. Let the arms move naturally with you.

step one:

- Step forwards on the right foot for count 1.
- Tap the left foot directly in front of the right foot, and lean the body back slightly on count 2.
- Using the left foot step back for count 3.
- Tap the right foot directly behind the left foot, and lean the body slightly forward on count 4.
- Repeat Step One up to count 7.
- Jump the feet together on count 8.
- Repeat Step One but lead with the left foot.

feeling confident? Ask the children to find a partner and dance the Charleston opposite each other.

dance 74 the ballerina (KS1)

Ballet began at the courts of Renaissance Italy. It was developed in France and then became popular all over the world. It has evolved into many different forms and styles.

teaching tip
Make sure the children know what the term 'first position' means (if their feet were the hands of a clock they would be showing 10 to 2).

description: Ask the children to form a circle ensuring they can see you. Begin with the feet in first position with the heels touching and the toes turned out. Hands should be on hips.

step one:

- Bend the knees whilst keeping the heels on the floor on count 1.
- Stretch the knees pulling the legs tight on count 2.
- Bend the knees whilst keeping the heels on the floor on count 3.
- Stretch the knees pulling the legs tight on count 4.

step two:

- Stretch the right toe forward, bending the left knee on count 5.
- Jump onto the right foot and stretch the left toe forward on count 6.
- Jump onto the left foot and stretch the right toe forward on count 7.
- Jump both feet back to first position on count 8.

feeling confident? Ask the children to find a partner and join hands to dance the Ballerina together.

dance 75 the gipsy (KS2)

Throughout history, the Roma people have suffered from a great deal of persecution and prejudice. However, dancing was one of the few ways in which they were allowed to make a living and to express their identity. This dance is a tribute to their indomitable spirit.

description: Ask the children to find a space facing you. Begin with the feet together, and let the arms move naturally with you.

There are half counts in this routine counted 'and'.

step one:

- Using the right foot step to the right on count 1.
- Place the left foot behind the right foot on count 'and'.
- Using the right foot do a step in place on count 2.
- Clap the hands twice on counts 3, 4.

step two:

- Using the left foot step to the left on count 5.
- Place the right foot behind the left foot on count 'and'.
- Using the left foot do a step in place on count 6.
- Clap the hands twice on counts 7, 8.

step three:

- Using the right foot take three jogs turning clockwise for counts 1, 2, 3.
- Jump the feet together and clap the hands on count 4.
- Using the left foot take three jogs turning anti-clockwise for counts 5, 6, 7.
- Jump the feet together and clap the hands on count 8.

feeling confident? Dance the Gipsy in a circle, encouraging the children to try to move in unison.

dance 76 the maypole (KS2)

The Maypole dance is based on the traditional celebration of dancing round the Maypole on the first day of May.

> **teaching tip**
> Make sure the children remember to let go of each person's arm as they go round the circle!

description: Ask the children to form a circle ensuring they can all see you. Assign the letters A or B to each child. Make sure that the letters are alternate all the way around the circle. Ask all the As to face the left ready to move clockwise. Ask all the Bs to face the right ready to move anti-clockwise. The dancers pass alternately right and left of the dancers going in the opposite direction.

step one (for both As and Bs)

■ As you pass each person in the circle, angle your right shoulder to their right shoulder, then your left shoulder to their left shoulder.

■ Repeat this movement all the way round the circle.

step two (for both As and Bs)

■ Using the right foot take 32 springy skips to move all the way around the circle on counts 1–32.

feeling confident? Try linking arms with each person you pass – right arm to right arm, and left arm to left arm.

dance 77 quickstep (KS2)

The Quickstep is an English ballroom dance that, as its name suggests, makes use of quick stepping and syncopated feet rhythms in time to up-tempo music.

teaching tip

The basic feel of the Quickstep is slow-quick-quick, slow-quick-quick. The 'slow' steps are usually taken on the heel, while most 'quick' steps are taken on the balls of the feet or toes.

description: Ask the children to move over to the right side of the room as this dance will move towards the left. Begin with the feet together, hands on your hips.

There are half counts in this dance counted 'and'.

step one:

- Using the right foot take a long step forward and diagonally left on count 1.
- Using the left foot take a small step to the left on count 2.
- Bring the right foot to meet the left foot on 'and'.
- Using the left foot take another step to the left on count 3.

step two:

- Using the right foot take a long step back on count 1.
- Using the left foot take a small step to the left on count 2.
- Bring the right foot to meet the left foot on 'and'.
- Using the left foot take another step to the left on count 3.

feeling confident? Ask the children to find a partner and join hands. Partner A will remain facing forwards and dance the original routine. Partner B will face their partner and dance the routine in opposition beginning with the left foot moving back.

dance 78 tango (KS2)

The Tango comes from Buenos Aires in Argentina.

> **teaching tip**
> Clap and count out the music first: slow-slow-quick-quick-slow-slow, quick-quick-quick, quick-quick-quick.

description: Ask the children to move over to the right side of the room as this dance will move towards the left. Ask the children to turn and face the front left corner. Begin with the feet together, knees slightly bent, hands on your hips.

step one:

- Using the left foot first take six steps forward.
- This should be counted and danced: slow-slow-quick-quick-slow-slow.

step two:

- Have the right foot forward but with the weight evenly distributed.
- Rock the body weight back onto the left foot for count 1.
- Rock the body weight forward onto the right foot for count 2.
- Rock the body weight back again for count 3.
- This should be counted and danced: quick-quick-quick.

step three:

- Using the right foot step back on count 1.
- Using the left foot step to the side on count 2.
- Bring the right foot to meet the left foot on count 3.
- This should be counted and danced: quick-quick-quick.

feeling confident? Ask the children to find a partner and join hands to dance the Tango together trying not to look at their feet. Remember: The partner moving backwards will have to reverse the steps.

dance 79 the lindy hop (KS2)

Dance legend has it that the Lindy Hop got its name when Charles Lindbergh, the famous American aviator, became the first person to fly solo non-stop from New York to Paris in 1927. A newspaper headline of the time read: 'LINDY HOPS THE ATLANTIC'.

> **teaching tip**
> This dance involves the children kicking out their legs, so make sure they angle the kicks away from each other!

description: Ask the children to find a space in the room facing you. Begin with the feet together, knees slightly bent, let the arms move naturally.

This dance has half counts counted 'and'.

step one:

- Kick the right foot forward whilst hopping on the left foot on count 1.
- Replace the right foot down on count 'and'.
- Kick the left foot forward whilst hopping on the right foot on count 2.
- Replace the left foot down for count 'and'.
- Repeat Step One for counts 3, 'and', 4, 'and'.

step two:

- Kick the right foot to the right side whilst hopping on the left foot on count 5.
- Replace the right foot down for count 'and'.
- Kick the left foot out to the left side whilst hopping on the right foot on count 6.
- Replace the left foot down for count 'and'.
- Repeat Step Two for counts 7, 'and', 8, 'and'.

feeling confident? Ask the children to find a partner and join hands to dance the Lindy Hop together.

dance 80 the slow rhythm (KS1 and KS2)

There are three main rhythms in ballroom dancing. The first rhythm is known as a slow. A slow is equivalent to two beats.

> **teaching tip**
> This dance routine is counted: slow-quick-quick-slow-quick-quick-slow.

description: Ask the children to find a space facing you. Begin on the left side of the room as the routine moves towards the right. Begin with the feet together, hands on your hips.

This dance has half beats counted as 'and'.

step one:

- Using the left foot step back on count 1 (slow).
- Using the right foot step to the right on count 2 (quick).
- Bring the left foot to meet the right foot on count 'and' (quick).
- Using the right foot step to the right on count 3 (slow).

step two:

- Using the left foot step forwards on count 4 (slow).
- Using the right foot step to the right on count 5 (quick).
- Bring the left foot to meet the right foot on count 'and' (quick).
- Using the right foot step to the right on count 6 (slow).

Repeat Steps One and Two and you will continue moving to the right.

feeling confident? Ask the children to find a partner and join hands facing each other. Partner A will dance Steps 1 and 2, and Partner B will begin on the right foot stepping forwards on count 1. Partner B will continue the rest of the routine moving to the left.

FUN ROUTINES

The dance routines in this book have all taken their inspiration from some of the best-known and loved dances in the world. However, in this section, although many of the routines are based on familiar dances like the Cancan and the Hokey Cokey, they have all been created or chosen because they are weird and wacky and fun to do.

dance 81 the cheer (KS1)

This routine is inspired by those performed by cheerleaders at sports events. By the way, these days cheerleading is done by boys as well as girls.

---

teaching tip
The calling can either replace the music or be done with the music.

---

description: Ask the children to find a space facing you. Begin with the feet together, hands on hips.

- 'Ready Ok!' Roll the arms and put them back on your hips on counts 1, 2.
- 'Out!' Step the right foot and right hand out to the right on count 3.
- 'Out!' Step the left foot and left hand out to the left on count 4.
- 'In!' Bring the right foot and right hand back to centre on count 5.
- 'In!' Bring the left foot and left hand back to centre on count 6.
- 'Start' Jump into a crouch resting the hands on the floor on count 7.
- 'Again!' Jump back up and place the hands on the hips on count 8.

feeling confident? Divide the class into two groups and take turns at dancing the Cheer really loudly.

dance 82 the boxer (KS1)

This routine is an homage to the character, Rocky Balboa, the underdog hero of the *Rocky* movies.

description: Ask the children to find a space facing you. Begin with the feet together, use your arms to help you move.

step one:

- Take four jogs raising the knees up high on counts 1, 2, 3, 4.
- Alternating the right and left arms, throw four punches forward on counts 5, 6, 7, 8.
- Take four jogs raising the knees up high on counts 1, 2, 3, 4.
- Alternating the right and left arms, throw four punches forward on counts 5, 6, 7, 8.

step two:

- Jump down into a crouch on counts 1, 2.
- Jump back up and using the right and then the left arm, throw two punches on counts 3, 4.
- Jump down into a crouch on counts 5, 6.
- Jump back up and using the right and then the left arm, throw two punches on counts 7, 8.
- Repeat Step Two.

feeling confident? Ask the children to form a circle and dance the Boxer facing each other.

dance 83 conga (KS1)

The Conga is a Cuban dance. It was once considered so unruly that dancers had to obtain a police permit before being allowed to do it!

> **teaching tip**
> The children will need to make their steps smaller when dancing in a circle in the 'Feeling Confident' section.

description: Ask the children to form one line standing directly behind one another. Begin with the feet together, hands on the shoulders of the person in front.

step one:

- Using the right foot take three walks forward on counts 1, 2, 3.
- Kick the left foot out to the side on count 4.
- Using the left foot take three walks forward on counts 5, 6, 7.
- Kick the right foot out to the side on count 8.
- Repeat Step One.

step two:

- Using the right foot step to the right on count 1.
- Bring the left foot to meet the right foot on count 2.
- Using the right foot step to the right on count 3.
- Jump the feet together on count 4.
- Using the left foot step to the left on count 5.
- Bring the right foot to meet the left foot on count 6.
- Using the left foot step to the left on count 7.
- Jump the feet together on count 8.
- Repeat Step Two.

feeling confident? Ask the children to form a circle with their hands on each other's shoulders to dance the Conga in a circular motion.

dance 84 hippy shake (KS1)

This routine gives the whole body a workout – and not just the hips!

description: Ask the children to find a space facing you. Begin with the feet shoulder width apart, arms relaxed.

- Shake both hands eight times for counts 1–8.
- Shake both arms and hands eight times for counts 1–8.
- Shake both shoulders, arms and hands eight times for counts 1–8.
- Shake the upper body, both shoulders, arms and hands eight times for counts 1–8.
- Shake the hips, upper body, both shoulders, arms and hands eight times for counts 1–8.
- Shake the knees, hips, upper body, both shoulders, arms and hands eight times for counts 1–8.
- Shake the feet, knees, hips, upper body, both shoulders, arms and hands eight times for counts 1–8.

feeling confident? Isolate each body part and shake it individually trying not to move the others.

dance 85 mexican wave (KS1 and KS2)

The Mexican Wave first came to the world's attention when crowds at the 1986 football World Cup created a wave effect by standing up and down in succession.

> **teaching tip**
> Discuss with the children what a 'wave effect' is and how they are going to achieve it. NB. During Step Two, encourage each child to step forward as soon as the child before them has taken their second walk forward. This will give you a smooth wave.

description: Ask the children to form a long line facing you. Begin with the feet together, arms relaxed.

step one:

- Using the right foot step to the right on count 1.
- Tap the left toe behind the right foot and clap the hands on count 2.
- Using the left foot step to the left on count 3.
- Tap the right toe behind the left foot and clap the hands on count 4.
- Repeat Step One for counts 5, 6, 7, 8.

step two:

Starting at one end of the line and continuing down to the end, the children individually and one after the other, do the following steps to create a wave effect.

- Take three walks forward raising the arms forward and up on counts 1, 2, 3.
- Jump the feet together and clap the hands on count 4.
- Take three walks back lowering the arms downward on counts 5, 6, 7.
- Jump the feet together and clap the hands on count 8.
- Repeat Step Two.

feeling confident? Don't wait too long between children walking forward at Step Two. Try to make the movement seem like a real wave.

dance 86 train (KS1)

This routine is based on the dance hit The Loco-motion. Loco is the Spanish word for 'crazy'. Now, asking a whole group of children to act like a train may indeed seem a little crazy, but they will have fun doing this dance.

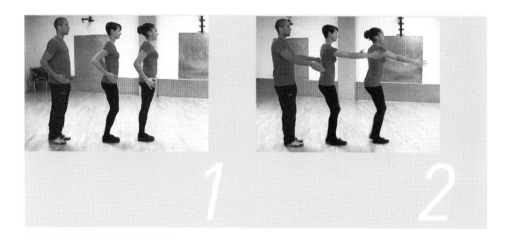

---

teaching tip

For the train effect to work, it's vital to get the children to move their arms and legs in unison.

---

description: Ask the children to find a space facing you. Begin with the feet together, knees slightly bent, arms relaxed.

- Using the right foot step forwards lifting both arms up on count 1.
- Bring the left foot to meet the right foot pushing arms forward on count 2.
- Using the right foot step back pushing arms down on count 3.
- Bring the left foot to meet the right foot pushing the elbows back on count 4.

feeling confident? Ask the children to form a 'train' standing one behind another. They can dance the Train routine together using the steps to move forwards.

dance 87 the vogue (KS1 and KS2)

This stylised dance routine is intended to mimic the poses made by models on the catwalks at fashion shows.

> **teaching tip**
> Get the children to really think about the poses they strike. Encourage them to combine different levels and spaces, for example, arms high straight above the head (high level, narrow space); arms spread out, knees bent (wide space, low level).

description: Ask the children to find a space facing you. Begin with the feet together, and use your arms to help you walk.

step one:

- Using the right foot take three walks to the right on counts 1, 2, 3.
- Strike a pose: place the right hand on the hip and the left hand in the air on count 4.
- Using the left foot take three walks to the left on counts 5, 6, 7.
- Strike a pose: place the left hand on the hip and the right hand in the air on count 8.

step two:

- Using the right foot take three walks forward on counts 1, 2, 3.
- Strike a pose: step the left foot forward and cross the arms on the chest on count 4.
- Using the left foot take three walks backward on counts 5, 6, 7.
- Strike a pose: step the right foot back and stretch both arms out to the side pointing the fingers on count 8.

feeling confident? Ask the children to spend some time thinking about four poses of their own. Dance the Vogue incorporating these positions.

dance 88 cancan (KS1 and KS2)

Believe it or not, there are reliefs from the time of the Ancient Egyptians that depict dancers high kicking in the style of the Cancan! The dance as we know it today was first made popular in Paris in the 19th century.

teaching tip
Make sure the children remember to let go of each other before completing the last move of the routine.

description: Ask the children to find a space facing you. Begin with the feet together, hands on the hips.

- Jump in place on count 1.
- Keeping it straight, kick the right leg forward on count 2.
- Jump the feet together on count 3.
- Keeping it straight, kick the left leg forward on count 4.
- Jump the feet together on count 5.
- Keeping it straight, kick the right leg forward on count 6.
- Jump the feet together on count 7.
- Keeping it straight, kick the left leg forward on count 8.
- Repeat.
- At the end of the music: jump down onto the right knee and reach both arms up into the air.

feeling confident? Ask the children to form one line and put their arms around each other's waists. They should try to stay in time to the music and in unison with each other.

dance 89 the clapper (KS1 and KS2)

This routine is very useful for children who need more practice with rhythm and timing.

description: Ask the children to find a space facing you. Begin with the feet together, arms relaxed.

step one:

- Clap the hands together four times on counts 1, 2, 3, 4.
- Using the right foot stamp out to the right on count 5.
- Using the left foot stamp out to the left on count 6.
- Slap both knees with both hands on counts 7, 8.

step two:

- Clap the hands together four times on counts 1, 2, 3, 4.
- Stamp the right foot back to the centre on count 5.
- Stamp the left foot back to the centre on count 6.
- Slap both knees with both hands on count 7, 8.

feeling confident? Ask the children to find a partner and dance the Clapper together.

dance 90 — the footballer (KS1 and KS2)

Not everyone can be a premiership footballer and earn thousands of pounds a week, but everyone can have fun doing this footballer routine!

> **teaching tip**
> This routine entails a good deal of kicking out by the children so make sure they have plenty of space in which to perform it.

description: Ask the children to find a space facing you. Begin with the feet together, use the arms to help you jump and kick.

step one:

- Kick the right foot forward on count 1.
- Jump onto the right foot and kick the left foot forward on count 2.
- Jump onto the left foot and kick the right foot forward on count 3.
- Jump onto the right foot and kick the left foot forward on count 4.
- Repeat Step One for counts 5, 6, 7.
- Jump with the feet together on count 8.

step two:

- Using the right foot take three jogs to the right on counts 1, 2, 3.
- Jump up, bringing the feet together, and head an imaginary ball on count 4.
- Using the left foot take three jogs to the left on counts 5, 6, 7.
- Jump up, bringing the feet together, and head the 'ball' on count 8.

feeling confident? Ask the children to form a circle and dance the Footballer together.

dance 91 hokey cokey (KS1 and KS2)

This routine is a version of the old favourite the Hokey Cokey. The best way to introduce it to the children, who may not be familiar with it, is to sing it and do the actions at the same time! You can do this with or without the music. However, if you do decide to use the music, be aware that the moves may be sung in a different order to the order specified here.

teaching tip
When the children walk into the circle holding hands, make sure they do so in a controlled way and don't collide with each other.

description: Ask the children to form a circle. Begin with the feet together.

Put your right hand in, your right hand out,

In out, in out and shake it all about.

Do the Hokey Cokey (shake the hands) and turn around.

That's what it's all about (join hands with each other).

Oh! The Hokey Cokey (Walk into the centre and back out again).

Oh! The Hokey Cokey (Walk into the centre and back out again).

Oh! The Hokey Cokey (Walk into the centre and back out again).

Knees bent, arms stretched, rah rah rah (clap the hands together three times).

Repeat the above putting your left hand, right foot, left foot and whole self into the centre.

feeling confident? Try to do the Hokey Cokey in silence. Challenge the children to remember correctly the sequence of the actions.

dance 92 musical statues (KS1)

The term 'freestyle' means that the children can make up any dance movement they choose.

---

teaching tip
In the competitive version of the routine, allow children who are out to continue freestyle dancing at the side of the room, and keep those still in the competition at the centre.

---

description: Tell the children to find a space in the room.

- Ask the children to freestyle their own moves to the music.
- Encourage them to move high and low, fast and slow.
- Tell the children to stop dancing when the music stops and restart when the music begins again.

feeling confident? Make the game competitive by saying that the last child to stop dancing is out. You can also play this dancing game by sitting down when the music stops.

dance 93 upside your head (KS1)

This routine is inspired by the funk music of the late 1970s.

description: Ask the children to find a space facing you. Begin with the feet wide apart, arms outstretched.

There are half counts in this dance counted 'and'.

step one:

- ■ Push the right arm down and the left arm up, bending the body over to the right on counts 1, 2.
- ■ Push the left arm down and the right arm up, bending the body over to the left on counts 3, 4.
- ■ Repeat Step One for counts 5, 6 and 7, 8.

step two:

- ■ Clap the hands twice on counts 1, 2.
- ■ Punch the right hand out to the right twice on counts 3, 4.
- ■ Clap the hands twice on counts 5, 6.
- ■ Punch the left hand out to the left twice on counts 7, 8.

feeling confident? Ask the children to sit on the floor one behind the other with their legs stretched out to both sides to dance Upside Your Head sitting down.

dance 94 the workout (KS2)

This aerobic routine should be danced vigorously.

---

teaching tip
You can make this a really demanding workout by adding new moves to the routine and cumulatively building up the number of steps.

---

description: Ask the children to find a space facing you. Begin with the feet together, and use the arms to help you move.

step one:

- Using the right foot first take eight marches on the spot for counts 1–8.
- Using the right foot take a large step out to the right and bend the knees deeply on counts 1, 2.
- Bring the right foot back to the centre on counts 3, 4.
- Using the left foot take a large step out to the left and bend the knees deeply on counts 5, 6.
- Bring the left foot back to the centre on counts 7, 8.
- Repeat Step One.

step two:

- Raise the left knee up to the right elbow on count 1.
- Replace the foot down on count 2.
- Raise the right knee up to the left elbow on count 3.

- Replace the foot down on count 4.
- Repeat Step Two for counts 5, 6, 7, 8.
- Take one deep squat for counts 1, 2, 3, 4.
- Repeat the squat for counts 5, 6, 7, 8.

feeling confident? Add extra moves to the routine, but make sure they are in time to the music.

COOLING DOWN

We are all aware of how important it is to warm up properly before taking vigorous exercise, but it is equally important to allow time for cooling down afterwards. Cooling down will help prevent any injuries and allow the children to bring their bodies back to their normal resting state. These activities should be accompanied by calming, soothing music.

calf and hip stretch (KS1 and KS2)

During dancing, muscle fibres, tendons and ligaments in the children's calves and hips will naturally become stressed. This cool down is designed to help reduce that stress and any lactic acid that may have built up in their bloodstream.

---

teaching tip
Do this stretch slowly – don't bounce.

- Begin the stretch standing up.
- Take a big step forward with your left foot.
- Bend your left knee (but don't push it beyond your left foot).
- Keep your right heel on the ground and your right leg straight behind you.
- Let your arms hang loose at your sides.
- Don't arch your back.
- Feel the stretch in both your right calf and hip.
- Hold for six deep breaths.
- Now switch legs and repeat.

dance 96 wall stretch (KS1 and KS2)

The children will feel the stretch in the muscles of their upper arms and chest.

> **teaching tip**
> To stretch more muscles in their upper arms and chest, the children can move their hand position either higher or lower and then repeat the Wall Stretch.

- Ask the children to place the palm, inner elbow, and shoulder of one arm against a wall.
- Tell them to breathe out slowly whilst turning their bodies away from the wall, still keeping their arms against the wall.
- Change arms and repeat the stretch.

dance 97 | hands above head stretch (KS1 and KS2)

The children will feel this stretch in their shoulders as well as their arms.

- Tell the children to interlock their fingers.
- Raise the hands above the head with the palms facing upwards.
- Slowly breathe out whilst pushing the hands further above your head.

dance 98 thigh hug

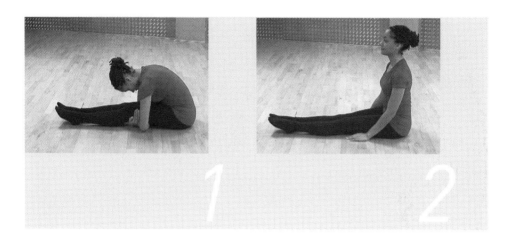

---

teaching tip
The children should keep their feet extended out and their knees together as they pull their chest down onto the tops of their thighs.

- Sit on the mat.
- Breathe out slowly.
- Bend forward.
- Put both arms under your thighs.
- Hug your thighs.
- Hold the position for a few seconds.
- Let go of your thighs and sit back up slowly.

dance 99 prone stretch (KS1 and KS2)

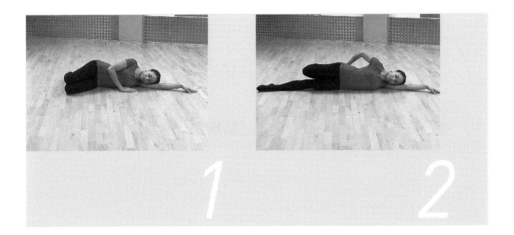

---

teaching tip

The children have to lie down on the floor to do this stretch so make sure there are mats provided for them.

- Have the children lie down on their sides with their legs bent.
- Tell them to keep their knees and the inside of their thighs together.
- Keep the top leg bent.
- Grasp the foot of the top leg with one hand.
- Stretch the lower leg out straight.
- Breathe out slowly and pull the foot gently towards the bottom.
- Slowly push the pelvis forward.

dance 100 leg stretch (KS1 and KS2)

---

teaching tip
While engaged in this stretch it's important that the children keep their heads and bottoms in contact with the mat at all times.

- ▓ Have the children lie on their backs on a mat.
- ▓ Slowly lift one leg upwards.
- ▓ Hold the leg with both hands around the calf or the hamstrings (or a combination of both if that makes it easier for the children).
- ▓ Keeping the leg straight, pull it toward the chest.
- ▓ Relax the stretch a little by contracting the muscles of the thigh (the quadriceps) on the same leg.
- ▓ Gently lower the leg to the floor.
- ▓ Repeat the stretch using the other leg.

dance 101 toe grab (KS1 and KS2)

teaching tip
Hold this stretch for a slow count of 20. Tell the children to take deep breaths in through their noses, and out through their mouths.

- Begin this stretch sitting down with your heels together.
- Hold both feet with your hands.
- Lean forward slowly from your hips.
- Gradually increase the stretch by bringing your heels closer to your groin and your chest closer to your feet.
- Make the movements small and controlled.
- Don't put too much upward pressure on your feet.